The Upholstery Bible

The Upholstery Bible

Complete Step-by-Step Techniques
for Professional Results

Cherry Dobson

D&C
David and Charles

A DAVID & CHARLES BOOK

David & Charles is an F+W Media, Inc. company
4700 East Galbraith Road
Cincinnati, OH 45236

First published in the UK in 2009

ISBN–13: 978-0-7153-2937-5
ISBN–10: 0-7153-2937-5
QUAR.TUB

Conceived, designed and produced by
Quarto Publishing plc
The Old Brewery
6 Blundell Street
London N7 9BH

Project Editor: Ben Hubbard
Art Editor: Jacqueline Palmer
Designer: Louise Downey
Art Director: Caroline Guest
Illustrators: Kuo Kang Chen, John Woodcock
Photographer: Paul Forrester, Simon Pask
Picture research: Sarah Bell

Art Director: Moira Clinch
Publisher: Paul Carslake

Manufactured by SC(Sang Choy) International Pte Ltd., Singapore
Printed in Singapore by Star Standard Industries Pte Ltd for David & Charles
Brunel House, Newton Abbot, Devon

Visit our website at www.davidandcharles.co.uk

David & Charles books are available from all good bookshops; alternatively you can contact our Orderline on 0870 9908222 or write to us at FREEPOST EX2 110, D&C Direct, Newton Abbot, TQ12 4ZZ (no stamp required UK only); US customers call 800-289-0963 and Canadian customers call 800-840-5220.

Dedication

To the memory of my father Harry Cook, who endowed me with his practical skills, and my late husband Roger, whose spirit has been ever present over my shoulder during the preparation of this guide.

Contents

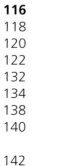

Foreword

The restoration and reupholstery of furniture has recently been enjoying a revival. This new appreciation has been fuelled by an admiration of traditional quality, the wonderful variety of fabrics available and the desire of people of all ages and backgrounds to embark upon projects with pleasing and worthwhile objectives. This guide will help to lead you through the basics of the craft, but also introduce you to some of my personal "tips", which come from many years' experience of tackling the "knotty problems" that frequently occur in upholstery. The craft is labour intensive and requires patience and perseverance – but the rewards are wonderful. I hope that this book will be a useful addition to your bookshelf and will encourage you, so that you will both enjoy and take pride in the results.

Acknowledgements

To my mother for her love and patience when I have been engrossed in the "book". To my many friends who have been so supportive, especially to Peter for his diligent proof reading, and to Pat for providing the food. Not forgetting the students I have met over the past 25 years. Without them and their chairs, I would never have learned so much. Hopefully this book will be a reminder to all of them of the techniques I have taught them.

About this book

This book is a complete course in upholstering furniture, including tooling up, selecting stuffings and outer textiles, techniques and cutting plans.

Tools and materials
(pages 12–31)

Starting with the basic tools, this section gives an overview of the equipment you'll need, including springs, stuffings and textiles.

Identification guide

Identifies and illustrates the upholsterer's kit.

Techniques
(pages 33–115)

Most of the techniques are demonstrated on chairs but the same principles can be applied to larger pieces of furniture in need of upholstery.

Tools and materials listing

At each stage, the tools and materials you will need are listed.

Supplementary diagrams

Diagrams supplement the photographic information.

Types of furniture

This part identifies what lies beneath the "skin" of different types of furniture. No two pieces of furniture are identical: use this section as a guide to plan how to measure your project and how to cut fabric to minimize the quantity you have to buy. In many cases, cutting plans are provided for both plain and patterned fabric.

Cross references

The techniques required to upholster a similar piece are listed here.

Taking measurements

Diagram illustrates the important measurements needed to plan how much upholstery fabric to purchase.

Key

In this section, the following abbreviations are used. Here, metric measurements precede imperial measurements.

I = inner
O = outer
A = arm
B = back
Shaded area = waste or piping

Measurement chart

Chart identifies the number of pieces and their dimensions for the featured item of furniture.

Cutting plan

The cutting plan shows the shape and dimensions of the pieces to cut laid out on a length of fabric, 137 cm (54 in.) wide.

ARMCHAIR VARIATIONS

Horseshoe chair with curved back
Castors allow the chair to roll smoothly. Look for a cream velour or green leather, to show off the rosewood legs.

Key features

Labels identify key aspects of the featured piece of furniture from an upholstery point of view.

Variations

Illustrates furniture style variations and suggests upholstery options.

Upholsterer's Order of Work

1. Find a piece of furniture to upholster. If you are a beginner choose something simple, such as a chair with a drop-in seat.

2. Strip the furniture (pages 34–39), making a note of the materials that have been used and how they were applied.

3. Apply the webbing (pages 40–45) to create a platform for the stuffings.

4. Check the condition of the springs and either reuse or replace them (pages 46–57).

5. Add hessian to cover the springs (pages 58–67).

6. Apply the first layer of stuffing (pages 68–79).

7. Apply a stitched edge for shape retention (pages 80–85).

8. Apply a second stuffing of hair (pages 86–91).

9. Measure and cut the new coverings and apply (pages 92–97).

10. Add buttoning if required (pages 98–102 and 104–105).

11. Add the finishing touches, such as piping, braid, gimp and studs (pages 112–115).

12. Finish the piece with lining underneath the chair to conceal the workings of the upholstery (page 113).

The upholsterer's art

Traditional methods of upholstery are still used today despite the invention of synthetic fibres. Upholstery is a skilled craft requiring judgement and dexterity and every piece of furniture needs to be approached differently. The stuffing is built up gradually following the contours of the frame and the upholsterer has to judge whether the shape and height look and feel right.

An ornate French armchair, from the reign of Louis XVI. With upholstered seat, back and arm rests. This is the work of a famous Paris-based master upholsterer called Georges Jacob (1739–1814).

Early upholstery was rudimentary. Girthweb – the type of webbing used for making saddle girths – was woven across the frame and tacked at the edges. In France it was close-woven, but elsewhere there were large gaps between the girths. The webbing was then covered with a piece of hessian or coarse sackcloth and some form of padding was piled on, either feathers, wool, animal hair or vegetable matter such as straw, chaff, rushes or dried grasses and leaves. Occasionally the padding was roughly secured with bridle ties before the top cover was nailed on. The backs of chairs were usually stuffed with washed and curled real hair, which was more expensive, stitched onto a linen or canvas backing. After about 1660 real hair was used to a much greater extent and the front and sometimes the sides of the seats, which received the greatest wear, were strengthened with an extra band of stuffing sewn into a roll of hessian or canvas.

Additional layers of fabric, usually wadding or linen, were placed between the real hair and the top cover to prevent the hair from working its way through the fine fabric above. Some chairs had loose cushions filled with down or feathers.

In the eighteenth century these techniques were refined, and complicated curved and straight-edged upholstery was carefully moulded by more precise stuffing and stitching. Often there were two layers of stuffing on the seat – one thin layer of real hair above a thicker layer of cheap vegetable fibre. Sometimes the padding was held in place with stitching or with regularly spaced ties that gave the surface of the upholstery a slightly indented pattern. This is now called shallow buttoning or tufting because silk tufts and not buttons were used as a decorative finish to each tie. In France, tufting was described as capitonné. Buttons did not replace the ties until the end of the eighteenth century. Until the middle of the eighteenth century, the upholstery of a chair or sofa was its most important part and often cost more in materials and workmanship than the frame. Consequently the upholsterer, or "upholder", was held in high esteem. In France the two crafts of tapissier (upholsterer) and menuisier (chair maker), were kept entirely separate.

The upholsterer often supplied all the textile furnishings of a house, from the elaborate wall hangings and curtains down to simple pillows and mattresses. As an interior designer, advising his clients on their choice and arrangement of furnishings, he probably had a greater influence on the final appearance of a house than the architect who designed it. (Most upholsterers were also undertakers and supplied the accessories that decorated the funeral cortège and the elaborate black curtains and ornaments that decorated a house during mourning.)

A modern armchair with foam padded seat and back.

Seats get more comfortable

Deep buttoning resulted from the widespread use of the coiled spring after 1820, which greatly deepened the padding. This springing was the only major advance in upholstery technique for over a century. The addition of a layer of springs underneath the layers of stuffing allowed the upholstery to move slightly and therefore made it more comfortable. The backs as well as the seats were often sprung and the thicker stuffing needed to cover the springs was prevented from slipping by the deep-set buttons. The resulting pleating of the material became a decorative feature and buttoning sometimes appeared on the arms too, though they were not always themselves sprung.

At first, springs were attached at the bottom to wooden planks, i.e. similar to modern ready-made wood and metal sprung units, which simply slot into the frame. These were soon replaced by more flexible webbing.

Between 1650 and 1800, real hair was used for the padding, but as it became more expensive, other materials were used to pad it out. These have included coconut fibre, known as coir or kerly fibre, various coarse grasses and leaves, cotton, rags and wool waste, and even wood chippings. The 20th century saw the introduction of rubber webbing, staple guns, latex and polyurethane foam.

Tools and Materials

Tools can be purchased through a local supplier or over the Internet. Using the correct tools ensures that each job is done efficiently and professionally. Equally important are the textiles you choose: whether you are going classic or contemporary, buy a textile that combines beauty and quality. You want to create pieces that can be admired and used. The examples here give an idea of what professional upholsterers can achieve.

Basic tools

As a beginner you will need the basic tools to strip your project of its coverings, tacks and staples. But before this you must consider your workspace. Take into account the area you work in including the walls. Develop a workroom plan so you have enough space to lay out and cut fabric as well as somewhere to store your materials. You will also need to have your furniture on trestles or an adjustable bench at the correct height for you to work comfortably. Make sure you have an adjustable chair to minimize backache.

The following pages illustrate the tools and equipment you will need as a beginner, but also tools and machinery for professional upholsterers. Many upholstery tools are the same as they were a century ago, although today they are available in different shapes and sizes. It is up to the upholsterer to decide which tools they find the most useful, as most people have tools they favour and others they seldom use. The basic tools that you will need in your tool box, are: a wooden mallet, a ripping chisel, a tack- or staple-remover, pincers, sharp scissors, a webbing stretcher, a magnetic hammer, regulators, a tape measure, needles, pins and skewers. A more experienced or professional upholsterer may also need: an industrial sewing machine, a buttoning machine, a glue gun and an electric or pneumatic stapler.

Finding and accessing furniture

Furniture that is suitable for renovation can come from a variety of sources. The auction room, antique shop or eBay are the most obvious places, but usually the amateur begins with a piece they already own. Before buying furniture to upholster, examine it for woodworm (small bore holes in the wood) to check the frame is solid. The shape and style of the chair usually indicate its age and quality, although faults can be hidden under a layer of upholstery. Normally, a good quality chair is made from a hardwood like mahogany, walnut or rosewood, which can be seen on the legs or any other show wood on the chair. The shape of the chair legs is also a telling feature – they should be substantial, and not spindly in appearance. The back legs should be made from the same wood as the front, and have an outward or ogee (double) curve. Castors should be made from brass, with china or brass wheels.

Tools: the basic kit

1. A wooden mallet is used in conjunction with a ripping chisel to remove tacks. Use a wooden mallet or a barrel-shaped wooden mallet. Do not strike the chisel with a metal hammer because it could damage its handle.

2. A ripping chisel has either a straight (a) or cranked (b) shaft and is used to lever out tacks. It is used in conjunction with a wooden mallet. Do not use a sharp-edged chisel as you will damage its sharp end when levering out the tacks.

3. A tack remover is used to remove tacks and dome-headed decorative nails used on leather upholstery. It is particularly useful for removing temporary tacks when adjusting the tension of fabrics. Removers may have wooden (a) or plastic (b) handles.

4. Magnetic hammers come in several types – the most popular is the two-headed hammer (a and b) with a magnetic head at one end for picking up and holding tacks, and a larger head at the other end for hammering. A hammer with a rubber end (c) is for hammering tacks into soft or fragile woods.

5. A slot and peg webbing stretcher is used to stretch the webbing tightly over the chair frame. As an alternative use a gooseneck webbing stretcher, which catches the webbing close to the frame.

6. Staple removers come in many types. The blade puller (a) is best for removing staples from fabric and soft wood; and the pronged-end types (b and c) are better for prising staples from hard woods.

7. Sharp scissors are a must. Keep two pairs – a general pair for cutting twine, rubberized hair and wadding, and the other solely for fabrics. Scissors should be a minimum length of 20 cm (8 in.) for trimming; 25 cm (10 in.) – or more depending on the size of your hands) for cutting the fabric. It is essential that the fabric scissors have sharp tips so that cuts can be made accurately.

8. Pincers are needed to remove tacks that have lost their heads. They can also be used to pull out stray staples, or remove the nibs of staples that break off.

9. Staple guns vary from the flat-bedded hand-tacker, to the preferable pneumatic or electric gun with a nozzle. Make sure you use the gun's correct-sized staple. The gun should be able to fire staples of the following lengths: 5 mm ($\frac{3}{16}$ in.); 10 mm ($\frac{3}{8}$ in.); 13 mm ($\frac{1}{2}$ in.).

❋ UPHOLSTERER'S TIP
Don't buy cheap scissors – buy the best quality you can afford. Because they will be used in your workroom for a variety of cutting and trimming tasks, it is essential that you keep your scissors sharp and in good condition. You will need a minimum length of 20 cm (8 in.) scissors for trimming, and 25 cm (10 in.) scissors for cutting the fabric.

9

4 a

5

7

4 c

8

4 b

3 a

3 b

2 a

6 c

1

2 b

6 b

6 a

2 a

Tools: the basic kit continued

1. Regulators come in several lengths, with a sharp point at one end and a blunt end at the other. The longer length – the 20 cm or 25 cm (8 in or 10 in.) – is used for distributing hair evenly under calico, and the shorter 15 cm (6 in.) is very useful for applying top fabric, because the blunt end helps to form neat pleats and tucks.

2. Double-pointed needles are used with twine to form a stitched edge. Needles with a bayonet tip are used when a cutting edge on the needle is required.

3. Skewers are available in two lengths: 7.5 cm (3 in.), and 10 cm (4 in.). They are used for holding fabric in place before it is sewed or tacked down. Pins are available in 2.5 cm (1 in.) lengths, and are also used for holding fabric in place.

4. Large curved needles are used for attaching springs and sewing bridles into hessian. The smaller 7.5 cm (3 in.) curved needles are used for slip-stitching top fabric; and the larger 10 cm (4 in.), or 12.5 cm (5 in.) curved needles for any stitching involving heavier fabrics, such as hessian.

5. A tape measure and metrestick (or yardstick) are used for measuring the chair and estimating how much fabric is required. A soft tape measure, shown here, is used for measuring the fabric components on chairs, and a metrestick is used for measuring and marking fabric prior to cutting.

6. Wax chalk (not shown) for marking fabric for cutting. Wax chalk does not rub off too easily.

Webbings and springs

Webbing is used as the foundation for furniture. A strong seat requires a strong base, with properly spaced webbing that will even the weight and diameter of the springs used. There are several types of webbing made from jute, linen, cotton or rubber. When reupholstering, use webbing similar to that originally used on the chair. Stretch the webbing across your frame using a webbing stretcher to form a sound base for the subsequent materials. Always use good quality webbing and never reuse the old webbing, which will almost certainly be past its sell-by-date. Springs are an integral part of traditional upholstery, and while not all seating must be sprung, springs do add depth and comfort that you don't always get with just padding and foam. Your choice of spring will depend on the piece you are upholstering. If you replace springs, use the same type used in the original upholstery.

Springs

1. Tension springs are more commonly used on fireside chairs and are fixed with clips or hooked into a webbing or metal plate with eyelet holes. The springs should be stretched across the frame of the chair and measure 2.5 cm (1 in.) less than the width of the frame.

2. Coil springs are used in traditional chairs and come in a variety of heights and gauges. The firmer No. 9 or No. 10 springs are used on the seat, and the softer No. 12 springs are used for the backs. The number of springs used depends on the size of the seat. A dining chair, for example, would have four 12.5 cm (5 in.) No. 10 gauge springs, whereas a large armchair would have nine 17 cm or 20 cm (7 in or 8 in.) No. 9 gauge springs.

3. Zigzag springs are used for all modern upholstery. They are attached by clips across the frame of the chair from back to front and, for the professional upholsterer, are a quick and easy type of spring to apply.

Webbing

4. Black and white webbing (with a double chevron weave) is the best quality but also the most expensive. It usually comes in a 5 cm (2 in.) width, and is used on traditional chairs.

5. Jute is the next best alternative to black and white and is the webbing most commonly used.

6. Rubber webbing is used on modern chairs to replace tension or zigzag springs, and to form a base for a seat upholstered with foam or rubberized hair. It is stretched across the chair frame and held in place with either clips or staples.

7. Heavy rubberized elastic webbing is used as an alternative to rubber webbbing.

Materials

Materials and fabrics are anchored and attached to furniture with tacks, staples or gimp pins, using a hammer or staple gun. Tacks can be bought in boxes of 100 gm (3½ oz.), or small packets and staples in boxes of 2,500.

1. Laid cord is used for lashing down springs. It has very little stretch and is made from hemp, flax and jute. It is available in 250 gm (9 oz.) or 500 gm (18 oz.) balls.

2. Twines and cords are made from flax, jute and hemp and come in graded sizes 1 to 4. Waxed twines made from flax are stronger than those made from other fibres, and are recommended for all upholstery work. Nylon twine is cheap and good for buttoning, and can be used instead of laid cord to tie down springs. Twines come in 250 gm (½ lb) balls. No. 3 is a good all round twine to use.

3. Piping cord is commonly made from cotton and makes piping. It can be natural or pre-shrunk. Use the pre-shrunk type to make cushions that will be washed. The thickness of the piping cord depends on the type of fabric used.

4. Staples come in sizes similar to the tacks above. Longer staples are used for webbing and hessian, and short ones for calico and top covers.

5. Cut or blue tacks come in two basic types: fine and improved. Fine tacks have a small head and are used on fabrics with a close weave, such as top fabric or calico. Improved tacks have larger heads and are used on loose-weave fabrics such as webbing, hessian, and scrim. They come in the following lengths: 16 mm (⅝ in.) improved tacks for webbing, and for anchoring spring ties; 16 mm (⅝ in.) fine tacks for webbing where the wood is liable to split; 13 mm (½ in.) improved for hessian; 13 mm (½ in.) fine tacks for tacking through thicker layers of cloth; 10 mm (⅜ in.) improved tacks for attaching scrim when constructing a stitched edge; and 10 mm (⅜ in.) fine tacks for attaching calico and top coverings.

6. Decorative nails are patterned with a brass or bronze finish. They can also be coloured and are used individually to anchor the top fabric.

7. Nail strips are used to cover the cut edges of leather or vinyl furniture.

8. Domed nails are plain with either a brass or bronze finish and are used for close nailing or attaching a nail strip.

Gimp pins (not shown) are small, fine, coloured tacks, which come in 10 mm (⅜ in.) and 13 mm (½ in.), and are used to attach braid and gimp. They can also be used as a final fixing to coordinate with the top fabric.

Stuffings, fillings and foam

When a piece of furniture is stripped, its stuffings are revealed. Throw away the waddings, but keep the hair and fibre, unless the strands of hair have broken into small pieces. The hair can be placed in a pillowcase and washed by hand or in a machine. You can use hair from an old mattress if it is of good quality. When purchasing stuffings, it is worth buying the best you can afford.

There are several types of animal hair available to buy, ranging from the common hog- and horse-hair, to the more expensive white cattle tail. Ginger coir and black fibre are very good alternatives and much cheaper. All of these are available to buy from upholstery suppliers in 13 kg (28 lb.) bags. Whatever type you choose to use, hair needs to be covered with wadding to make a smooth surface and prevent the strands working their way through the top cover.

There are three main types of wadding: white cotton wadding, blue wool, and polyester wadding. Polyester wadding is usually used on top of white cotton wadding to make an even, smooth finish; on top of foam as a protective cover; or as a lining, before the finishing fabric is attached to the outside arms and back. It is available in several thicknesses and widths, and rolls vary in length between 10 m (33 ft) and 50 m (164 ft). Modern fillings are foam and rubberized hair. Rubberized hair looks a little like real hair, but strands are coated with rubber latex and bonded together, almost to the consistency of a foam sheet. It is available in 2.5 cm (1 in.) and 5 cm (2 in.) thick sheets, in sizes 92 cm (36 in.) by 183 cm (72 in.). Foam is found on most modern chairs, settees, and headboards and is available in varying grades and thicknesses depending on its use. A good supplier will help advise on which type is best for your project. It is not a cheap option for stuffing, however – the price of foam 5 cm (2 in.) thick is twice the price of that 2.5 cm (1 in.) thick.

Types of stuffings

1. Black fibre is made from shredded leaves that are curled and dyed, and is cheaper than animal hair, although the dye does come off on your hands. Black fibre is used as a first stuffing on chairs and settees and is useful in forming a stitched edge.

2. Animal hair is available to buy in hessian sacks, although it is expensive. It comes in varying qualities but the cheapest one is fine to use. It is used for a first stuffing on drop-in seats, or pincushion seats where there is only one stuffing – or as a second stuffing on other furniture.

3. Ginger coir or coconut fibre is also used as a first stuffing and is useful for forming a stitched edge.

4. Rubberized hair is a good alternative to foam, hair or coir stuffing on chair seats or backs and is fire retardant. It is easily moulded and provides a more traditional feel than foam stuffing. Weight: 1150 gm (36 oz.), 183 cm x 92 cm (size 72 in x 36 in.) Thickness: 2.5 cm (1 in.) or 5 cm (2 in.).

5. Cotton wadding is also known as white cotton wadding. It is made from pure new cotton that has been layered. There are two weights available, the thinner one is suitable for general upholstery. Fire-retardant waddings are also available. The two weights are: 750 gm (26.5 oz.), width 68 cm (27 in.), length 17.5 m (19 yd); 1200 gm (42.3 oz.), width 68 cm (27 in.), length 11 m (11.9 yd). This wadding is used to cover hair, coir or fibre to make a smooth finish and to prevent the hair working through the top cover. It is also used on its own as a pad for simple upholstery.

6. Woollen felt/blue wadding comes in two types: layered or needled. It is made from woollen waste, which is woven together. The layered type falls apart easily and is not recommended, but the needled type is strong and useful for covering rubberized hair followed by a covering of white cotton wadding. It is also used as a covering for springs in sprung cushions.

7. Skin wadding is a thin wadding with a cellulose surface. It is used as an additional covering to white cotton wadding and provides a very smooth finish. Skin wadding is available in 32's and 52's. (no-one seems to know what these numbers relate to). 32's: width 18 in (46 cm), length 20 m (21.5 yd); 52's: width 46 cm (18 in.), 10 m (10.8 yd).

8. Polyester wadding is used as an additional covering for white cotton wadding to give a smooth and luxurious feel to the upholstery. It can also be used on the outside of chairs, as wadding between the hessian and top fabric. It is available in 2 widths: 69 cm (27 in.), or 137 cm (54 in.); and comes in various thicknesses from 70 gm (2.5 oz.) to 475 gm (16 oz.). The thinnest type is adequate for most upholstery, and the thicker one is normally used only for cushion interiors.

9. Foam (left) comes in different grades and thicknesses, as chip foam and also as latex, which is more expensive. It is available in large sheets or in pieces cut to the exact size and shape required. When using foam, consider its use and how it will be supported in the frame, and always cover it with a protective layer, like stockinette or polyester wadding. Otherwise the millions of small holes in the foam can pluck the threads of the finishing fabric. All foams sold for furniture in UK must be fire resistant.

Feathers (not shown) are used as a cushion filler. The feathers can be mixed with down to form a more deluxe filling and come in 25 kg (55 lb.) sacks. Feather cushions can be custom-made, which is preferable, as stuffing a cushion with feathers can prove both difficult and messy.

9

Pincore latex   **Reconstituted chip**   **Common foam**

Coverings and linings

There are many different fabrics used when recovering traditional furniture. As illustrated, start with the hessian base and work your way through the layers to build a strong foundation for the proper sequence of coverings and linings.

1 & 2. Hessian is used on top of webbing or springs to act as a base for the hair stuffing, and can be found on traditional or modern pieces of furniture. Hessian is available in three different weights – 213 gm (7.5 oz.), 273 gm (10 oz.), and 366 gm (12 oz.) – and is usually 18.3 m (72 in.) wide. The 366 gm(12 oz.) is the best quality and should be used at all times if available.

3 & 4. Scrim is another form of hessian that is like cheesecloth – it has a very loose and airy weave, and is often used for cheap curtains. It is used when a second stuffing and a stitched edge are required on a chair. The evenness of its weave makes stitching an edge easier. It is available in No. 2 or No. 7. qualities. No. 2 is the thickest, with a higher number of yarns to the inch. No. 7 is a looser weave cloth and is used similarly to the No. 2, but is easier to use where the frame has a curve. Both of these scrims are available in a 72 in (183 cm) width. A superior quality scrim is made from linen – this only comes in a 36 in (92 cm) width.

5. Calico (sometimes known as cotton duck) is used to cover and tighten the stuffings that have been applied to a chair. Use calico underneath a top fabric as it takes the strain before the top fabric is applied. Calico will also hold the stuffing in place if the cover needs to be changed. Use good quality calico where possible and take care if it has been treated for fire retardancy, as the fabric can be very brittle and easy to tear. It is often better to use an untreated calico and then a barrier cloth on top to conform to fire retardancy requirements.

6 & 7. Platform lining is a strong cloth that comes in various colours and is used on seats underneath loose cushions. However, this makes the cushion non-reversible. In its black form it is used on the underneath of chairs to neaten and act as a dust barrier.

8. Cambric is a strong cotton fabric used to make cushion pads. It is wax-proofed to prevent feathers and down working their way through the fabric.

9. Blue and white ticking is also used for making cushion interiors and traditionally is a twill weave and blue and white.

10. Stockinette is a knitted fabric that comes in rolls, and is used for covering foam cushions. It is easy to apply although the raw edges at the ends of the cushion need to be overlocked.

5 6 7 8 9 10

Textiles

There are a number of different textiles to choose from when upholstering a piece of furniture. Your choice of textile will depend on a number of factors – primarily the piece of furniture you are upholstering, but also its use, the room it is going into, and of course your own personal style preferences. Most people know what they like when they see it. But if you take a minute to learn how to define your style preferences, you'll be more likely to find exactly the furnishings you're looking for.

CHOOSING A STYLE

"Style" is a very personal thing. You may love the smooth, sleek lines of contemporary pieces, or you may prefer the traditional charm of furnishings from the eighteenth century. That's the beauty of home furnishings – there's so much to choose from that it's easy to find the pieces that express your unique style.

It is helpful to know the basic style category you're looking for; it gives you a great place to start. To help you focus in on a "look", browse through your favourite magazines to find pieces or entire rooms that appeal to you. Tear out the pages and take them with you when you shop. Whether it's a sofa, loveseat, chair or ottoman, upholstered furniture usually falls into one of the following main style categories:

Traditional

This term refers to that designed with a deliberate adherence to the past. It is by far the largest of the style categories, with a dozen or more sub-categories ranging from Italian Renaissance to Louis XV or Queen Anne, and Chippendale to Art Deco. Traditional styles are more conservative – perhaps even formal – and feature a wealth of elegant details, such as symmetrical designs, graceful carved curves, rich and mellow colours, dark polished woods like cherry and mahogany, and fine upholstery. Think of European antiques,

wingback chairs, camelback sofas, damask, jacquard and chintz fabric covers, and Oriental influences. These are good examples of what "traditional" styling is all about.

Velvet, chenille, mohair or maybe even corduroy, these plush fabrics are inviting and long-wearing.

Transitional

These designs blend influences from a variety of old and new style categories. As a result, the overall look is much more up-to-date than pure traditional styles. Transitional designs, since they usually incorporate both traditional and contemporary elements, are more versatile with regard to interior decorating. Furnishings with transitional styling are easy to coordinate, creating a casual, easy-going look. These styles are more understated, and cater to today's laid-back lifestyles. This is the world of overstuffed sofas, easy-care "performance" fabrics, solid colours, and lighter-finish woods that

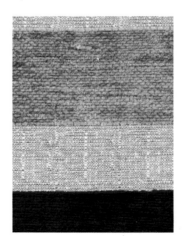

will help you to create warm, relaxed interiors that favour neutral colours and soft textures, and make for an inviting look. Picture a loft apartment – light and airy, high ceilings, sleek furniture designs upholstered in neutrals, with artwork, collectables, pillows and cushions bringing in bright colour splashes.

The cranberry stripe at the bottom of this bold design will add colour and warmth to an otherwise neutral room.

Contemporary

The term contemporary covers several styles of furniture that were developed in the latter half of the twentieth century. It's not "modern", but it is an updated look with sleek, rounded lines, and clean, crisp shapes. Contemporary is considered to be a fashion-forward, upscale design look that favours simplicity and a minimalist approach – the focus is on function and efficiency. Fabrics lean towards textures and weaves in solids, stripes and prints. Colours may be neutral, or bold with striking patterns. Leather is a popular upholstery choice for contemporary designs. (Accessories may lean

towards metal and glass.)

One of today's most popular upholstery looks is "casual contemporary". It still features lean lines and strong silhouettes, but is much more relaxed, allowing a warmer, more comfortable look.

This polka dot fabric would go well on a Morris chair with a leather seat.

Eclectic

Eclectic interiors are highly individualized and feature a diverse mix of compatible styles. For example, an antique armoire might be paired with a contemporary sofa and chair, with occasional tables that are similar, but don't match. Accents might include objects

collected from around the world, unusual artwork, or pieces with whimsical or sentimental value. In eclectic room designs, furniture and textured fabric covers typically cross styles and periods, while colour is often the common denominator. True eclectic style can be as distinctive and beautiful as any other category.

Soft colours, like the duck egg blue in this floral design, are ideal for neutral schemes.

Slipcover

Also known as the "slipcover look", this style has a tailored cover that slips on and off for a comfortable, lived-in look (see photo, right). Slipcover styles enable you to change the look of an entire room simply by changing your furniture covers. "True" slipcovers come all the way off for dry cleaning or spot cleaning.

If you're having difficulty figuring out which style is the right one for you, don't despair. Lots of people are "hybrids" when it comes to decorating preferences. When designing a hybrid room, a good way to compromise is to pick a dominant style and then add accent pieces and accessories in a different style. Remember that the number one rule in decorating is: if you like it, it's right. Mix and match, and express yourself.

Remember that fabric "grade" is not an indication of quality or durability; it's just an indicator of how expensive the fabric is to make. Read the details on the fabric label attached to your swatch and make your decision accordingly.

Regardless of colour, fibre, thread count, or grade, upholstery fabrics should always be chosen to serve your needs, whether they be fashionable or practical. There are countless choices to be made, so don't settle for anything you're not in love with. Most importantly, be sure to pick a fabric that you can truly live with. And, if you grow tired of it in a few years, remember that virtually all upholstered furniture can be re-covered.

HOW TO CHOOSE AN UPHOLSTERY FABRIC

Nothing has a greater effect on the look of upholstered furniture than the fabric. It is the most visible indicator of both fashion and quality, but also the part of an upholstered piece to show soil and wear fastest. When selecting fabric, you must know what to look for and what questions to ask. With some basic considerations, you'll be able to recognize the differences between fabric types.

STYLE: The fabric should be appropriate to the style and character of the piece it is covering. A traditional frame will usually look best with a more traditional fabric style. Consider the scale of the pattern – this should be appropriate to the size of the room. As a rule, large repeating patterns look better in larger rooms. Also consider whether the fabric colour is cool or warm, and be sure it fits the "mood" of the room it will go into.

FADE RESISTANCE: Will your furniture be exposed to constant direct sunlight? To reduce the chances of fading, see if your choices include fabrics that are sunlight resistant. Here's where the synthetics make a very loud case for textiles that aren't just for boats any more!

DURABILITY: Will the furniture be in an area of the house where there is heavy traffic? Pieces subject to daily heavy wear need to be covered in tightly woven, tough and durable fabrics. Generally speaking, fabrics that have their pattern "woven in" wear better than printed fabrics.

COLOUR: This is probably the most influential factor when selecting a fabric, but a specific colour may not be the best choice for durability and stain resistance. If your household has small children and/or pets, you're probably better off choosing a colour that won't show dirt easily.

TAILORING: Fabric covers should be pulled tightly and contain no snags, unwanted tucks or dimples. Checked and plaid patterns should always be aligned and matched.

FORM AND FIBRE: When shopping for fabrics, you'll discover a vast array of different patterns, textures, thread counts, and fibre contents from which to select. But your choice will come down to natural fabrics, synthetics or a mixture of the two. Opposite is a rundown of some of your options:

NATURAL FABRICS

COTTON – This natural fibre provides good resistance to wear, fading, and pilling, but is less resistant to soiling and wrinkling. Surface treatments and blending with other fibres often compensate for these weaknesses. Durability and suitability for use will depend on the weave and finish of the fabric: damask weaves are formal, while canvas weaves such as duck and sailcloth are more casual and durable. Cotton is absorbent and feels cool against the skin in warm climates. Heavier weight cottons such as denims wear well, while polished ones, such as chintz, tend to weaken and split in just a few years.

COTTON BLENDS – Depending on the weave, cotton blends tend to be sturdy, family-friendly fabrics. For everyday use, it's a good idea to apply a stain-resistant finish (or look for fabrics which have already been treated, i.e. "Scotchguard").

LEATHER – Perhaps the best all-around upholstery fabric ever! Even though it can be expensive, leather may be a wonderfully rugged choice for your particular project. This tough material comes in many colours and finishes, and develops more softness and character with age. Leather is very forgiving, and easy to clean and maintain.   When buying leather for upholstery, go to a reputable hide supplier. If you must, buy "splits", but you may be sorely disappointed in the quality and durability of the leather.

SILK – This beautiful, delicate fabric is suitable for adult areas, such as formal living rooms or bedrooms. It must be professionally cleaned if soiled. For successful upholstery use, silk must be "cotton backed" – this is an additional process done by a lamination service before the fabric is cut and sewn. If you do select silk for your upholstery/curtain project, do not place the furniture in an unprotected sunny location – silk will last for a very long time, but the direct sun will cause it to rot in a few short years.

WOOL – Sturdy and durable, wool and wool blends offer good resistance to pilling, fading, wrinkling and soiling. Generally, wool is blended with a synthetic fibre to make it easier to clean. Blends can be spot-cleaned when necessary.

SYNTHETICS

ACETATE – Developed as imitation silk, this fabric resists mildew, pilling and shrinking, but is not a good choice for furniture that will get everyday use.

ACRYLIC – This fabric was developed as imitation wool and resists wear, wrinkling, soiling and fading. Better quality acrylics are manufactured to resist pilling.

MICROFIBRE – This term is used to describe a new category of upholstery fabrics with a velvety, suede-like surface, also known as faux suede. Made from ultra fine polyester fibres, microfibre fabrics are durable and pleasant to the touch. These fabrics are of excellent value, durability and cleanability.

NYLON – Rarely used alone, nylon is usually blended with other fibres to make it one of the strongest upholstery fabrics. It is very resilient; in a blend it helps to eliminate the crushing of napped fabrics, such as velvet and chenilles. It doesn't readily soil or wrinkle, but it does tend to fade and pill.

OLEFIN – A popular, durable choice for furniture likely to receive heavy wear: "bullet proof" comes to mind when thinking of this textile. Contract grade fabrics very often use olefin for long-range projects.

POLYESTER – An attractive choice, rarely used alone in upholstery, polyester is blended with other fibres to add wrinkle resistance, eliminate crushing of napped fabrics (velvets, chenilles), and reduce fading. It neither stretches nor shrinks.

RAYON – Developed as an imitation silk, linen and cotton, rayon is durable, however, it does wrinkle. Recent advances have made high-quality rayon very practical for upholstery.

VINYL – Easy care and less expensive than leather, vinyls are ideal for busy family living and dining/eating areas, but remember: durability depends on quality.

Fabric families

1. Linen: twice as strong as cotton, and second in strength to silk, linen is an extremely durable natural fibre. However, it is not the obvious choice for the upholsterer, as it lacks the elasticity of cotton blends, is difficult to manipulate and wrinkles easily. These samples are 100 per cent linen, dry clean only, shown here in raspberry and sable.

2, 3, 4, 5, 6. Cotton blend: a cotton blend can consist of various different fibre types, in varying quantities, but a good quality cotton blend will advertise cotton as its principal ingredient. The blends here range from 45 per cent cotton, 45 per cent linen, 15 per cent nylon (top left), to 60 per cent cotton, 40 per cent modacrylic (centre right), to the less reliable 65 per cent viscose, 18 per cent cotton, 15 per cent linen, 2 per cent silk (far left).

7. Velvet blend: dense and heavy, velvet is very difficult to wash, so use a sensitive dry clean only. Rayon, cotton and polyester are common to most blends, but ideally velvet should be made from silk. A small percentage of Lycra is sometimes added to give stretch. The sample colours shown here are: (from left to right) aubergine, off white, cranberry and biscuit.

8. Polyester: 100 per cent polyester (as shown here in gold, brown and natural) is not suitable for upholstery as it resists shrinking and stretching. However, blended with other fibres, polyester is the perfect upholsterer's fabric as it is easy to clean and does not fade.

9. Faux suede: faux suede is a type of leather with a napped finish. Soft yet pliable, suede is a popular choice for upholstery. Make sure you treat it as a delicate: suede is prone to fading and is easily soiled. The sample colours here are: (from left to right) gold, brown, lichen and azure.

10. Leather: tough, long-lasting, and versatile, leather can bring real character to your upholstery. Leather is available in a variety of different finishes and colours, but it is often difficult to get your hands on large quantities, and you will find it expensive.

11. Silk blend: Silk is best for upholstery when it is cotton-backed, like these examples, which are 64 per cent cotton, 36 per cent silk. Be warned: silk is highly flammable.

12. Wool blend: These wool swatches are blended with linen (76 per cent wool, 24 per cent linen), making the wool base easier to clean, and introducing a soft colour and feel to the material.

Trimmings

Trimmings include gimps, braids and decorative cords that come in many different forms varying in colour, size and price. Both functional and decorative, trimmings can be used to add a bold accent, cover or disguise a stitched or tacked edge, enhance a frame's shape, lend an extra dimension to the furniture or simply as a form of traditional decoration.

Trimmings are used on a chair or settee to cover the raw edges and tacks on the top cover, and also to protect the fabric from fraying. They also give the chair a finishing touch, and can be attached with glue, gimp pins or stitching, depending on whether they are covering a line of tacks and a raw edge of fabric, or whether they are sitting on top of the fabric and hiding a stitched seam. Using a hot-glue gun is normally preferable, but care should be taken to keep the glue away from both the fabric and your fingers.

Trimming types

1–2: This type of braid has a flat edge one side and a scalloped edge on the other, and is often more expensive than a scroll gimp or flat braid. This braid can be used either way depending on the finish required.

3–5: Inexpensive gimp with a scroll edge on both sides. The multicolouring of the gimp means different effects can be achieved, depending on which way the gimp is applied.

6: Scroll gimp with a wavy edge on both sides. This type of gimp has a loose weave which makes it good for chairs with curves and corners.

7–8: Inexpensive decorative braids that aren't good for curves or corners.

9–10, 16: Alternative braids in varying widths and colours. These are not as commonly used as the scroll gimps shown above.

11–15: A range of decorative cords in various colours and widths. Cords can be hand-stitched onto fabric either to hide a seam or for decorative effect.

17–18: Two types of decorative cord with flange. Cords such as this are sewed into the seams, usually on cushions. Use a piping foot to apply these cords, and keep stitching very close to the cord.

A lime green trim is used to spike this raspberry coloured sofa, picking up the colours in the lampshade and cushions.

Techniques

What will distinguish your finished piece
will be the shape and condition of the
original item, the chosen textile – and
how that suits the furniture and the
interior in which the furniture is to be
placed – and the skill and craftmanship
that you have used in your reupholstery
work. This section walks you through the
techniques that you need to master.

Tools and materials

- **Ripping chisel:** To be used in conjunction with a mallet for levering out tacks and staples

- **Wooden mallet:** For striking a chisel, tack or staple remover

- **Tack remover:** To lever out prominent tacks

- **Staple remover:** To remove staples

- **Pincers:** To remove tacks and staples

- **Scissors**

- **Tape measure**

- **Notebook** and **pencil:** For taking notes as you complete the upholstering process

- **Garbage bags**

- **Camera:** For taking photos of the chair as it's stripped

- **PVA (craft) wood glue**

- **Upholstery apron:** Use an apron with pockets on the front to hold your tools, such as a tape measure and scissors

- **No. 2 wire wool**

- **Wadding pad**

- **Cleaner** or **methylated spirit**

- **Tourniquet** or **cramp**

- **Wood adhesive**

- **Face mask**

Stripping

Before a piece of furniture can be upholstered, it needs to be stripped of its old coverings. Prepare to be surprised; once materials and stuffings are exposed you can estimate the age of the piece. At this point, make a list of the replacement materials you'll need so the real business of upholstering can begin.

Late Victorian or early Edwardian armchair
The chair is upholstered in cotton velvet with coordinating figured velvet on the front of the back and cushion. Decorative fringing has been sewn along the bottom edge to cover the legs.

The piece of furniture you upholster may be a simple stool or chair, or it may be a large settee with cushions. Whatever the piece, the order for stripping remains the same – it's the upholstering process in reverse. So start with the covering underneath and work inwards.

Preparing a chair for stripping

First, you must decide what sort of surface you will work on to strip your chair. Trestles with a fixed wooden tray on the top are ideal, but make sure they are at a comfortable working height. Stripping can be a very dirty task, so wear an apron to protect your clothes from inevitable dust.

It's good working practice to have a camera and notebook at hand to take photographs and notes as you strip the chair. These will be useful to look back on and remind you what the piece looked like before stripping began, what stuffings were used and how they were applied.

When stripping, take care not to damage the surface wood that shows (show wood), with the sharp tools. Take note of the state of the frame and check if any of the joints are wobbly.

If wobbly, the joints can be knocked apart with a mallet and re-glued. If the wood is rotten or damaged then you will need to find a furniture restorer to repair the damage. If dirty, the show wood may be cleaned using either methylated spirit or a proprietary cleaner. The cleaning may be carried out at this stage, but the polishing is best left until immediately before attaching the final cover to prevent the polished finish from damage during the upholstering. (See pages 39 for cleaners and wood polishers.)

Upholstery materials

During the stripping process, make a note of the upholstering materials used as they are a good indication of what you'll need to replace them. The types of stuffing used will depend on the age of the chair, and should be replicated as closely as possible. Antique and old chairs usually have traditional stuffings, using some or all of the following: cotton or wool wadding, hair, coir, black fibre, coil springs, hessian and webbing; all of which are attached to the piece of furniture using tacks.

Sometimes, it will be clear that the piece has been reupholstered or re-covered previously. Look out for signs of this, as the work may not have been of the best quality and the materials used not ideal. Old stuffings are usually very dirty and dusty and should be discarded, as the dust could work its way through the top or bottom cover.

Keeping a record

Take photos and notes of every stage of stripping your chair. It is equally important to take pictures of the pieces of fabric that have been used, and make a note of exactly where they came from on the chair. The abbreviations listed here can be used to indicate the approximate size and location of each piece of fabric.

Fabric abbreviations

Location of components	Abbreviations of fabric components
B Bottom	A Arm
C Centre	B Back
F Front	C Cushion
I Inside	S Seat
O Outside	F Facing
R Right	FF Front facing
L Left	W Wing
T Top	

For example, when a piece of fabric is removed from the right arm, it could be noted as "RA". The location always goes first. Make sure you apply the abbreviations as if you and the piece of furniture were facing each other, front on.

Stripping an armchair

Starting with the bottom cover of hessian, remove all the upholstery using a mallet and ripping chisel.

Continue to remove the upholstery until the sprung edge of the back and the springs on the arm are exposed.

What can be reused?

Material, stuffings and springs should be reused only if they are clean and in good condition. This all depends on the age of the chair, the amount of use it has had and where it has been stored.

It's not advisable to reuse tacks as they are often bent and have damaged tips, making it difficult to hammer them into the wood. Chairs that have a sprung edge on the front rail are attached to a cane; this should be retained if it's not damaged.

Modern chairs
Modern chairs (shown above and below left) are usually upholstered with foam, rubberized hair and polyester wadding, which are attached to the frame with staples.

✳ Upholsterer's Tip
Protective gear
When stripping an old piece of furniture, wear a mask to avoid inhaling the dust.

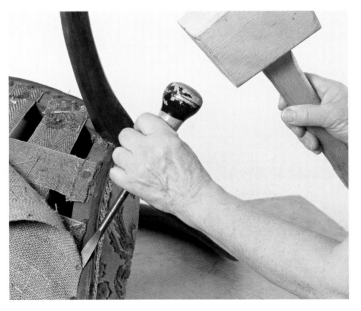

Reusing hair

You can wash and reuse hair as long as it has not broken up into small pieces. Clean it by hand in a bowl, or put it in the washing machine in a pillowcase carefully tied up with string. Then spread out the hair on an old sheet or towel and place flat to dry, either outside on a sunny day or inside in a warm place. Do not tumble dry – the hair will form tight balls that are difficult to tease out.

Out of shape springs
Discard coil springs like these out-of-shape examples (above). The springs should go up and down vertically and not bend over to one side. Similarly, discard tension springs that have lost their elasticity and become overstretched, or zigzag springs that have become unaligned.

REMOVING TACKS
Hold the chisel in your left hand and the wooden mallet in your right (reverse if you are left handed). Knock the edge of the chisel under the tack to remove it. Do not use a hammer because it will damage the chisel handle. When the edge of the chisel is under the tack's head, gradually lever the tack out of the wood. Old, rusty tacks sometimes break off, in which case it may be necessary to hammer home the remaining part of the tack to prevent further damage to the wood. Always knock the chisel in the direction of the straight grain of the wood to prevent the wood splitting.

Removing staples

There are several types of staple removers available – these are the three most common.

BERRY STAPLE REMOVER

The user-friendly handle and sharp, complex metal end makes this model the most efficient (and the most expensive) staple-removing tool.

SPADE STAPLE REMOVER

This is the cheapest model. When purchasing this tool, make sure the thickness of the spade end is suitable for the staple size.

OSBORNE STAPLE REMOVER

Reasonably priced, the Osborne is an effective tool, but the long handle may be a hindrance if you are stripping a chair with deep upholstery.

WORKING WITH THE MALLET

Using the staple remover in one hand and the mallet in the other, try to edge the point of the staple remover under the staple to wedge one of the legs of the staple into the groove of the remover.

If it breaks off, the remaining piece should either be removed with pincers or hammered in to prevent injury to your hand or damage to the upholstery.

Pincers
Use pincers to extract any snapped staples that may be left behind in the chair.

Use a rocking action to lever the staple out of the wood. The hardness or softness of the wood and the length of the staple will determine how easily the staple comes out.

❋ UPHOLSTERER'S TIP
When using a chisel, tack remover or staple remover, keep your free hand behind the sharp end of the tool, never in front. A chisel or staple remover can cause serious injury if it slips forward onto your hand.

Stripping the chair

Now that you have made the necessary preparations, it's time to strip the chair. The following steps will take you through the stripping process.

1 Once the bottom cloth and top fabrics of the seat have been removed, you will be able to assess the state of the upholstery. In this example, a wool wadding and a thin layer of skin wadding cover the second stuffing of hair. The scrim is rotten and so the pad is easily lifted from the tacks.

2 Using scissors, cut all the ties that hold the hair to the scrim and remove the entire pad from the seat. Note that the hair can be washed and reused.

3 Remove the hessian over the springs by carefully cutting the ties that hold it to the springs.

4 Remove the springs, webbing and all the remaining tacks from the chair frame using a tack remover and/or a ripping chisel and mallet.

Cleaning and repairing wooden frames

Clean any dust and dirt from the frame of the chair and examine to see
if any repairs are necessary. If any of the joints are loose, they can be
knocked apart and glued again. Fill any large tack holes with wood filler
and sand down when it has hardened.

1 If wobbly, the joints can be knocked apart with a mallet and reglued
using wood adhesive.

2 When gluing, make sure that the glue covers the whole dowel and that
there is only a small amount of glue in the dowel hole.

3 When reassembling, use a tourniquet or a clamp (with heads lined with
a protective lining such as fabric or cork) and apply medium pressure to
push the joint home.

4 Clean the show
wood with cleaner
or methylated spirit,
using No. 2 wire wool
and a pad of wadding.
This is to absorb the
liquid and prevent
it dripping on the
workbench.

Tools and materials

- **Jute webbing**

- **Black and white webbing**

- **Tape measure**

- **Sharp scissors**

- **Webbing stretcher**

- **16 mm (⅝ in) improved tacks**

- **Magnetic hammer**

- **Fibre-tipped pen**

Tacks

Tacks

The size of tacks used in upholstery varies between 6 mm to 16 mm (¼ in to ⅝ in) fine or improved. Large- headed improved tacks are used for loose-weave fabrics, while fine tacks are used for close weaves.

Hammers

Magnetic hammers are perfect for the job. They have a cabriole head and are easier to use than a small upholsterer's hammer. A magnetic hammer with a claw end isn't very useful as there is not a non-magnetic end with which to hammer the tacks.

Magnetic hammer

Webbing

Webbing is one of the basic principles of upholstery and is the base for all other stuffings on the seats, backs, and arms of traditional and modern chairs.

Types of webbing

There are several different types of webbing – jute and black and white are all made of natural fibres and do not stretch, while rubber webbing is designed to stretch and act as a sprung base. Jute and black and white are used on traditional chairs and rubber webbing is for modern pieces.

Whatever type you use, make sure it is of a good quality as it is the base for all the subsequent stuffings. It's generally not a good idea to reuse old webbing, as it is likely to be rotten and weakened from being stretched, while rubber webbing has a tendency to disintegrate.

Black and white webbing is three times more expensive than jute, which comes in varying qualities. The best jute webbing to use is 5.5 kg (12 lbs) and 5 cm (2 in) wide. This is the strongest jute available and usually has a coloured stripe down the middle.

Webbing a seat with springs

The webbing of chairs with springs, like this Victorian dining chair (right), should be attached on the underside of the frame so that the springs can be sewn in. Here, the webbing is woven in basket fashion: three strips from back to front, and three from side to side. They are attached using a webbing stretcher and secured with 16 mm (⅝ in) tacks.

Webbing a drop-in seat

This drop-in seat (right) has webbing attached to the top of its frame. Due to the wide seat shape, you will need to attach three strips of webbing from back to front, and three from side to side, woven in basket fashion. Use 16 mm (⅝ in) tacks, but if the wood is very hard (or has a tendency to split) then a smaller tack would be advisable.

Jute is the most common webbing used. It is reasonably priced and available in rolls of 33 m (108 ft). The quality of jute webbing is measured by its weight in pounds per 1 gross yard. 5.5–6.8 kg (12–15 lbs) is recommended. It comes in several widths but 5 cm (2 in) is the most widely used.

Black and white webbing has a double chevron weave and is usually considered the best webbing. It is more expensive but stronger and with less stretch than jute. It is available in 33 m (108 ft) rolls.

Rubber webbing (shown below) is used in modern chairs and designed to stretch. It is attached by clips or staples.

Where is the webbing attached?

It's easy to decide whether the webbing goes on the top or bottom of the chair frame: check to see if it has tack marks. If the wood underneath the chair is free of them and nicely polished, then the webbing goes on the top of the chair frame and the chair will have no springs. However, if the frame has tack marks underneath, this is where the webbing goes and springs will be used.

What type of tacks?

Always use blue or cut tacks, never bayonet tacks. Blue or cut tacks have a chamfered tip which goes easily into the wooden frame, while bayonet have a square parallel shank and are more like nails. They are available as "fine" or "improved" tacks. Fine tacks have smaller heads than improved tacks, and are used for close-weave fabrics, while improved tacks have large heads and so are used for loose-weave fabrics. 16 mm (⅝ in) improved tacks are most commonly used for webbing. They have a long shaft and a large head so that the head does not slip through the webbing. If the wood is very hard or delicate, then consider using the smaller 13 mm (½ in) improved tacks.

Checking for tack marks
Note the position of the large tack marks where the webbing was previously inserted. You will see that there were three vertical and three horizontal rows.

MARKING THE CHAIR RAIL

If the chair has not been webbed previously, it's a good idea to mark the chair rail with the proposed position of the new webbings using a fibre-tipped pen or chalk. The first mark should be in the centre of the rail with subsequent marks on either side working towards the legs. Markings should be directly opposite each other so that the webbings go in parallel lines.

HOW MANY WEBBINGS?

Position the rows of webbings in parallel lines, not more than 5 cm (2 in), or the width of the webbing, apart. Weave these lines from back to front and also from side to side in a basket-like fashion. It's always better to have too many rather than too few. On chairs that have an unusually shaped seat the webbings may be positioned at an angle, or go across diagonally.

Webbing the chair

Now you can begin to web the chair. Gather together your materials and tools (see page 40) and follow the steps below.

1 With the front of the drop-in seat facing you, place a roll of webbing on the floor or on your workbench. Fold over 2.5 cm (1 in) of the cut end of the webbing and place this end centrally, at the top back side of the frame.

3 Place the tacks in an up-down diagonal pattern, as in the diagram (right) and photograph (above).

Insert three tacks – one in the centre at the back of the fold and one on either side. Then add two more tacks in the spaces in front of these, to make two rows.

2 Using a magnetic hammer, insert five tacks in the webbing. Make sure you hammer the tacks into the centre of the frame and not near the edge, as this could cause the wooden frame to split. If the webbing is on the underneath of the chair, again ensure that it is positioned in the centre of the frame, or it may be in view.

4 Slip the piece of dowel (which can be attached to either side of the stretcher) through the loop of webbing.

USING THE WEBBING STRETCHER

5 Keep the chair in the same position so that the attached webbing is at the back. Pick up the webbing stretcher and hold it with the handle facing away from you, and the ridge underneath. Bring the webbing through the stretcher to form a loop.

The stretcher must be held correctly for the webbing to be stretched tightly. It's also important that the stretcher is used as in the picture above: with the webbing locked between the chair and the stretcher. Failure to do so lets the webbing slip and makes it difficult to get the tension tight.

Webbing stretchers

The slot and peg design (shown in the photograph below) or the gooseneck stretcher can both be used for this task.

✳ Upholsterer's Tip
Never cut webbing until it's anchored on both rails or you will be unable to thread it through the stretcher.

6 Pull the handle of the stretcher towards you to create tension on the webbing, and to keep it taut.

✳ Upholsterer's Tip
It's a good idea to mark the webbing stretcher in such a way that you will remember how to use it correctly. Green paint is used on the stretcher in the demonstration.

7 Again, pull the webbing stretcher towards your body, with the ridge of the stretcher under the chair frame and the webbing locked between the stretcher and the chair frame. The webbing will now be in a secure position and a high tension can be achieved. It should make a pinging noise when it's plucked.

8 Hold the stretcher firmly in your left hand to retain the webbing's tension. Insert three tacks into the webbing on the top of the front rail.

9 Cut the webbing, leaving about 2.5 cm (1 in) to turn over.

10 Remove the stretcher and fold over the tail of the webbing to the tack line. Hammer in two tacks to secure it. Now, repeat steps 1–10, positioning the webbing no more than the width of itself apart.

11 Without cutting the webbing, weave the end of the roll of webbing through the grid of webbings and tack down as before. Do not be tempted to tack down prior to weaving, as it is difficult to weave a whole roll of webbing through the grid.

12 Weave the webs in basket fashion. Now that all the rows of webbing are in place, you will have a strong base to which you can attach the rest of the upholstery.

✳ UPHOLSTERER'S TIP
Use the hammer to flatten the fold of the webbing.

Webbing a chair back

The procedure for webbing the back of a chair is very straightforward and follows the "webbing the chair" technique you have just learned.

To prevent the back of the chair sagging, first attach the webbing to the side rails on the back of the chair. Next, attach the vertical webbings to the front of the bottom rail – weave these behind the horizontal webbings and attach to the front of the top rail. The vertical webbings then prevent the horizontal webbings from bulging out at the back of the chair.

Sometimes webbings can replace chair rails that are missing, such as the rail at the bottom of the back, and the vertical rail at the back of the arm. Always note the angle of the webbing at the back.

Webbing a Chesterfield

The webbings on a Chesterfield are similar to a chair back. For a Chesterfield, the horizontal webbings go behind the vertical rails. Attach the vertical webbings to the front of the bottom rail, and then take these behind the horizontal webbings to the front of the top rail.

When stripping the sofa, take note of how the webbings were attached, as this pattern can then be repeated. If the sofa has already been stripped, then look for evidence of tack marks that indicate where the webbings would have been.

❋ UPHOLSTERER'S TIP
When attaching webbing to a side rail, use a stretcher, or a mallet, to support the rail.

Tools and materials

- **Springs:** That are suitable for the type of chair you are upholstering

- **Clips:** To anchor zigzag springs

- **Fixing bars:** To use with tension springs

- **Large staples:** For fixing tension springs on chair backs

- **Twine:** A good quality waxed twine for stitching the springs to the webbing

- **Laid cord:** A thick twine to lash down coil springs

- **16 mm (⅝ in) tacks**

- **Hammer**

- **Springing needle:** To stitch the coil springs to the webbing

- **Scissors**

- **Chalk** or **marker pen:** To mark the position of the springs

- **Wire cutters**

Springing

Springs are used in a chair, stool or settee to make it more comfortable or to make the seat higher. The three types most commonly used are coil, tension and zigzag.

Types of springs

The type of spring used in a chair depends on its size and whether it is a traditional or modern piece. Coil springs are the recognized springs for all traditional pieces but may also be used on modern pieces. Tension and zigzag springs are only used on modern furniture. Chairs and settees often have springs in the backs as well as the seats, but these are usually of a softer gauge, as they do not take the same wear as those on the seat.

Once you have removed the upholstery from a chair and the frame is bare, take a look underneath to see if there are any tack marks. If the wood is polished with no tack marks, then the webbing would have been on the top of the frame and the chair would have had no springs. If there are tack marks that indicate there has been webbing on the underneath of the frame, then the chair would have been sprung with coil springs.

Zigzag and sinuous springs

Zigzag springs (below) come in 30 m (100 ft) rolls in three different gauges, and are cut to length, using wire cutters, before they are attached. Anchor onto the top of the back rail of the chair with a clip, then tension to the front rail and anchor with another clip. These types of springs are used mainly on modern furniture because they are much easier and quicker to work with. They are covered with hessian, and then foam or rubberized hair, but in some cases hair or coir is used. Zigzag springs are attached to the rails of a chair with a clip which is nailed down.

Coil springs

Coil springs (below) come in different heights, ranging from 10 cm (4 in) to 30 cm (12 in), and in gauges ranging from 9 to 13, with 9 being the firmest. Coil springs are primarily used on traditional furniture – the softer ones on the backs of chairs and the firmer ones on the seat. Sew the springs to the webbing with thick twine and lash them with a thick cord to create a sprung seat – this prevents them going out of shape when used.

Coil springs are the most complicated to tie in and lash down, but are the recognized springs for all traditional chairs. Coil springs come in a variety of sizes and gauges.

10 cm (4 in) available in 12, 10 or 9 gauge

12.5 cm (5 in) available in 12, 10 or 9 gauge

15 cm (6 in) available in 12, 10 or 9 gauge

17.5 cm (7 in) available in 11, 10 or 9 gauge

20 cm (8 in) in 9 gauge

23 cm (9 in) in 9 gauge

25–30 cm (10–12 in) in 9 gauge

❋ UPHOLSTERER'S TIP
*Unless absolutely necessary,
never change the type of
spring in a chair. It will raise
all sorts of complications
whether the chair is
traditional or modern. It is
always better to keep to
the original type.*

Tension springs

Tension springs (below) are coated in either plastic or
fabric, and are usually used in modern wingback and
fireside chairs. They come in varying tensions – the softer
ones for use on the back of chairs, and the firmer ones
on chair seats. They are attached to the side rails of
the chair through eyelets in either a piece of fabric (as
shown right) or through a metal strip. If you remove the
springs, make sure you mark their position on the chair.

Fabric-covered spring

Fabric-covered spring

Plain, uncovered spring

*Tension springs are used on
the backs of chairs and are
hooked into a metal eye on
the rail of the chair.*

Spring units

Ready-made spring units (right) are
also available in various shapes and
sizes. Some have coil springs, which
are anchored to a steel frame with a
mesh top covering, others have soft
springs which are encased in calico
to form a pocketed cushion. Here,
the rows of springs are anchored
together with hog rings and the unit
is used as a cushion filling.

How to install coil springs

Coil springs are the most complicated springs to work with. The following steps will help you to insert and attach a coil spring. Decide on the quantity and gauge of springs you require. This depends on the type and size of the chair, but as a guide, the height of the springs should be approximately 2.5 cm (1 in) higher than the height of the finished seat.

1 Place the springs, making sure they are not less than 5 cm (2 in) apart and not too near the edge of the frame, or the seat will fall sharply at the edge. Arrange the springs symmetrically in straight rows. The knot on the top of the spring should be facing diagonally inwards, and ideally the bottom knot resting on a piece of webbing. The position of the top knot makes it easier to tie down and prevents the knot tearing the hessian which will eventually cover the springs.

2 Once you have decided on the position of the springs, make a mark around them on the webbing with chalk or a marker pen, so that if they move they can be easily replaced in the original position.

Choosing a spring for a project

Chair Back	Soft dining seat	Firm dining seat	Armchair
10–12.5 cm (4–5 in)	12.5–15 cm (5–6 in)	12.5 cm (5 in)	15–30 cm (6–12 in)
gauge size 12	gauge size 10	gauge size 9	gauge size 9–10

The five illustrations below show the arrangements of springs for small chairs, such as dining chairs and occasional chairs.

The spring arrangement on the left is for an armchair.

This arrangement below is for a chaise longue, which features a stretcher rail for added support.

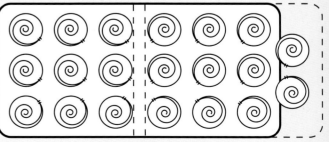

Stretcher rail

Stitching to webbing

Now that you have chosen the correct springs and arranged them, it's time to stitch them down. Using twine and a springing needle, stitch each spring with one stitch to the webbing in four places. Follow the steps below to complete this.

A slip knot underneath the webbing is an easy way to attach the twine. A slip knot is shown in detail on the right.

1 Start underneath the seat and bring the needle and thread up through the webbing, very close to the coil of the spring.

2 Now go over the coil and return the needle and twine through the webbing.

3 Attach the twine underneath the chair with a double slip knot.

4 Repeat steps 1 and 2, this time making a half hitch underneath. Remember to make sure that the twine is taut at all times. See a half hitch knot in detail below.

Pull the half hitch tight to secure the spring.

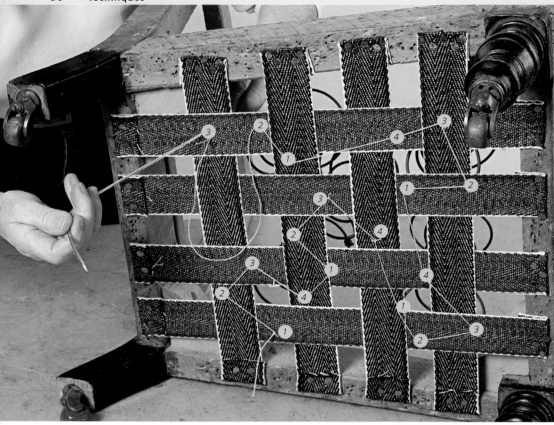

5 Repeat this sequence four times at equal distances around the spring, fastening each time with a half hitch knot (see page 49). Keep the twine tight and make sure that there are no loops in the twine between each knot. It should not be possible to twist or turn the springs once they have been secured to the webbing.

6 If the twine runs out before the process is finished, make a join with a reef knot (see page 55). To finish off, first make a half-hitch knot on the last spring.

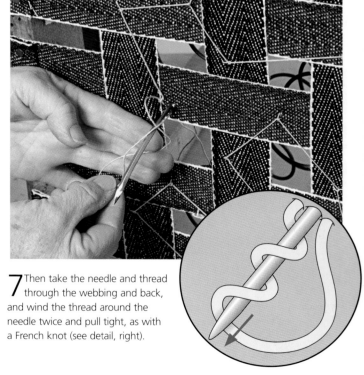

7 Then take the needle and thread through the webbing and back, and wind the thread around the needle twice and pull tight, as with a French knot (see detail, right).

Lashing the springs down

The springs must be lashed down to create a sprung unit. Failure to do so will result in a lumpy seat that goes out of shape very quickly. Follow the steps below to lash the springs down.

※ UPHOLSTERER'S TIP
As you lash the springs down, repeat to yourself: "Over the spring and underneath, over the string and through the loop".

1 Insert 16 mm (⅝ in) tacks at a 45-degree angle into the frame on the back, front and side rails, making sure they're aligned with the centre of the springs.

2 Measure a piece of laid cord one-and-a-half times the distance from the back to the front, or, if the springs are large, then twice the distance.

3 Now tie a slip knot in one end. Hook the slip knot over the tack at the back and hammer down securely.

4 Depress the spring at the back to the required finished height. Now place the cord over the spring and hold onto the top with your left hand.

5 Place the cord over and under the spring, taking the cord over the cord being held by your finger, and bring it forward through the loop to the right and pull tight.

6 Bring the cord onto the front of the spring, hold it securely with your left finger and thumb, then keeping a loop around your hand repeat the knot.

7 The distance between each spring on the top should be identical to the distance at the bottom. Repeat the knots at the back and front of each spring until you reach the front spring. With your left hand and arm, depress the springs to the required height and twist the cord around the tack at the front, tensioning it over the front rail to prevent the tack from coming out. Then hammer this tack home to anchor the cord.

8 Look at the position of the springs: they should be slightly tilted down to the sides of the chair but move up and down vertically when pressed. If they aren't in this position, the springs will become misshapen when the chair is used and make for an uncomfortable and distorted-looking seat.

9 Make a half hitch knot to secure the cord (see page 49).

10 Repeat this process from the back to the front on each row of springs and then across it from side to side. Again, springs should be slightly tilted to the outside rather than the inside. Hammer home the tacks that secure the cord.

Other sized springs

For springs 15 cm (6 in) or over, it may be necessary to make a second knot on the last spring. Make the knot in the middle part of the spring, and then take the twine around the tack on the front rail, and return to the top of the spring with a knot. This will prevent the spring from becoming distorted.

If springs are over 17.5 cm (7 in), then two rows of tying-down are required – the first one going through the middle of the springs, and the second row over the top. This helps greatly in the second tying-down and prevents the middle of the spring from going out of shape.

Tools and materials

- **Springs:** Use four for a chair, more for a sofa. Buy springs about 5 cm (2 in) shorter than the main springs and a No. 10 gauge.

- **Webbing:** To attach springs to chair frame

- **Laid cord:** To lash springs down

- **Edging cane or stout wire**

- **Twine:** To attach cane to springs

- **16 mm (⅝ in)** and **13 mm (½ in)** tacks

- **Clout nails**

- **Hammer and Scissors**

- **Marker pen**

Working a sprung edge

On large armchairs and settees with fully sprung seats, a sprung edge is necessary to make a firm edge to the seat. The springs should be approximately 50 mm (2 in) shorter than the main springs.

Creating a sprung edge

Place four or more springs on the front rail, anchor and tie them down, and attach to a piece of cane edge wire. Follow the steps below.

1 Place your springs on the front edge, positioning them between the rows of main springs, with one spring at either end of the rail. Use a marker pen to mark each spring's position.

2 Anchor the springs down with a piece of webbing threaded through the bottom of the spring. Tack each spring down on either of its sides, or anchor it with large staples onto the top of the front rail.

3 Measure a piece of laid cord to go over the spring from back to front, one and a half times, and attach it with a tack on the inside of the front rail. Depress each spring to the same height as the seat springs already in place – approximately level with the bottom of the arm – and tie a knot as before on the top of the spring (see page 52).

4 Make another knot on the top front edge of the spring and bring the cord through the spring. Anchor on the front of the rail with a large tack.

5 Take a piece of edging cane or stout wire of the width of the seat and hold it to the centre spring. Cut a length of twine of 91 cm (1 yd), attach the cane to the spring as in the picture and pull the twine tight.

6 Blanket stitch the top of each spring to the cane, one end of the twine going to the right and the other to the left.

7 Tie off in a reef knot (see detail, right).

8 In order to bring the springs forward a little, attach short pieces of webbing folded in half over the middle coil, and anchor down with tacks on the front of the seat rail in a "V" position. Use two or three 13 mm (½ in) tacks.

9 With a length of cord twice the width of the seat, make a tie from left to right going through the springs. Go up through the springs to the top in the middle, and then down to the other side. Anchor the tie at either end with a tack, and tie a piece of laid cord horizontally through the springs. Anchor with a tack.

10 Now that all the springs are anchored down securely, they are ready to be covered with hessian.

Other types of springs

Tension springs are attached to the top of the side rails of a chair by a standard metal plate with holes in it, or a fabric strip with eyelet holes.

Metal plates

Replace the metal plates if they are rusty and the holes worn. New plates can be obtained from an upholstery supplier and are easily attached with clout nails. Examine the fabric side fixings too, and if they show signs of wear or are rotten, replace them.

Attaching tension springs

The tension springs on a seat are attached to the side rails with a clip or staples. The seats of chairs are attached to the side rails. Different types of attachment are shown below.

1　　　　2　　　　3

1. The tension spring is hooked into the appropriate hole in the metal plate.
2. The spring hook is placed in the slot and fixed with a vertical nail.
3. The spring is placed on the hook inside the chair rail.

Spring pads

If the original springs are old or overstretched, they should be replaced. Ensure the new springs are 2.5 cm (1 in) shorter than the distance between the fixings so they are tight when stretched. To use them on a seat, cover them with a spring quilt or pad, and then a deep cushion. The spring pad is made from a piece of polyester wadding sandwiched between two layers of platform lining with a pocket at either end for the spring to be threaded through. This way, the cushion won't get worn by the springs.

Zigzag springs

Examine the clips that anchor zigzag springs and make sure they're not damaged. If the springs are overstretched, replace them. The springs are linked together with wire or twine, which should be intact. Replace the ties if worn or missing so the springs don't move side to side.

Tension springs

When tension springs are used on the back of a chair, they should be covered with a piece of hessian. This is to protect the subsequent stuffing from wearing under the movement of the springs. Subsequently, the hessian should be cut large enough to allow for a pleat to be made down the centre: this will account for any movement created by the springs.

Tools and materials

- **Hessian:** To form a base for the stuffings

- **Tacks:** 13 mm (½ in) improved and 16 mm (⅝ in)

- **Scissors**

- **Magnetic hammer**

- **Tack remover**

- **Hammer**

- **Tape measure**

- **Staple gun** and **staples**

- **Springing** or **12.5 cm (5 in) curved needle**

- **Length of twine**

- **Webbing**

- **Laid cord**

- **Wadding, hair, coir, foam** or **paper foam**

- **Foam tack roll**

Staple gun

Scissors

Preparing a hessian base

Hessian is a cloth used in upholstery as a platform to cover webbing and springs. It supports the stuffings that are later applied. This section explains how to apply hessian – first to seats without springs, and then to seats with springs.

Hessian is a stout cloth that comes in two qualities. The cheaper one has a loose weave, while the more expensive one is stronger with a tighter weave. The latter is preferable, because the closeness of the weave prevents hair and some dust from passing through it, and it's also more hard wearing.

✳ **UPHOLSTERER'S TIP**
When applying any fabric to a piece of furniture, ensure the grain of the fabric goes straight from the back of the chair to the front, and from side to side (as shown, right).

Applying the hessian to drop-in seats

Once the webbing is complete on the top of the frame, it needs to be covered with hessian so that the stuffings don't fall out of the chair.

1 Measure the seat top from the back to the front, and from side to side. Cut a square piece of hessian, allowing an extra 2.5 cm (1 in) around the square for turnings. Centre the fabric on the top of the back rail, and fold over 2.5 cm (1 in) along the raw edge.

2 Temporarily tack through the fold onto the top of the back rail using 13 mm (½ in) tacks. Apply three or four tacks about 5 cm (2 in) apart. Take care when tacking, and if the wood shows any signs of splitting, use a smaller and finer tack or a staple from a staple gun.

3 Repeat the tacking on the top of the front and side rails, but this time without folding the fabric over. Tack through the single layer of hessian and then repeat this on the side rails. Make sure the hessian is stretched over the webbing tightly and that the weave of the fabric is straight (both vertically and horizontally) when the chair is viewed from the front.

> ❊ UPHOLSTERER'S TIP
> *Always initially anchor the fabric in the centre of the four sides.*

4 When the hessian has been temporarily tacked all around the fabric and is taut, hammer the tacks home.

5 Fold the excess hessian over on the three remaining sides and tack down. Then neatly fold the corners on top of the frame.

6 Trim the excess fabric with scissors to neaten the hessian. This cut should be approximately 2.5–5 cm (1–2 in) from the tacks. The seat will now have a firm base and is ready for stuffing.

Stuffed over-seats with or without coil springs

Stuffed over-seats without springs have hessian covering the webbing, while seats with springs, such as the one below, have the springs covered with hessian. When measuring these seats allow extra hessian for covering the springs.

1 Set the hessian on top of the springs. Take care when tacking down that hollows do not form in the hessian between the springs: the hessian should just sit tightly on top.

2 Fold the hessian at the back and anchor with three temporary tacks. Using an upholsterer's hammer with a curved head is helpful here if the bottom rail of the chair's back is in your way.

3 With the hessian unfolded on the top, place three tacks at the front.

4 Place three tacks at either side to ensure that the grain of the hessian runs straight from front to back and from side to side.

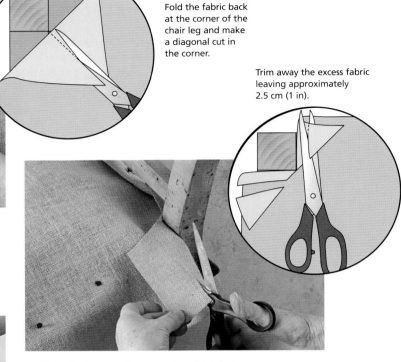

Fold the fabric back at the corner of the chair leg and make a diagonal cut in the corner.

Trim away the excess fabric leaving approximately 2.5 cm (1 in).

5 Having inserted several tacks on each side, the hessian must be cut to go round the back corners. At each corner, fold the material back and make a mark on the inside corner. Then make a cut diagonally across to this mark

6 Take the hessian either side of the back leg and fold back the excess. Trim this off leaving 2.5 cm (1 in) turning.

7 Trim the hessian all round the chair to within 2.5 cm (1 in) of the temporary tacks.

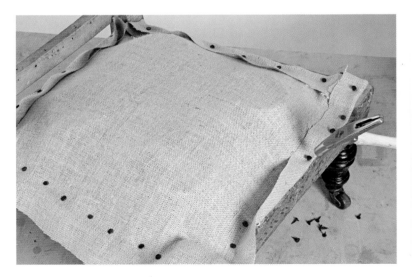

8 Add extra tacks where necessary about 5 cm (2 in) apart. When all the tacks are in place and the hessian sits tightly on top of the springs, hammer the tacks home.

9 Finally, fold the excess fabric over and tack down permanently.

Attaching the hessian to the springs

The hessian is stitched to the springs to stabilize its position and to ensure that all the subsequent stuffings are attached to the springs. Sew the hessian to the springs using a springing – or 12.5 cm (5 in) – curved needle and a length of twine.

1 Take the curved needle and thread from the top of the hessian, under the spring, and up through the hessian. Tie a slip knot on the top (see page 49).

2 Again, take the needle and thread through the hessian, under the spring, and back through the hessian, about a third of the way around the spring. Make a knot on the top.

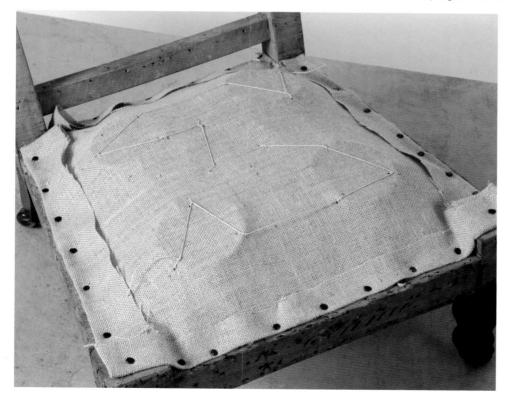

3 Repeat the process another third of the way around. Move to the next spring without tying off the twine. Repeat this process until all springs have been tied in. If the twine runs out, attach another length using a reef knot (see page 55).

Chairs with a sprung edge on front rail

The hessian on a seat with a sprung edge, such as the one below, covers the main springs and forms a well between the main springs and those on the front edge. When filled with hair, this well separates the main springs from the front sprung edge.

1 Tack the hessian with temporary tacks on the back, front and side rails, leaving the excess piece of hessian at the front. This will eventually go into the well behind the front edge springs. Sew the hessian to the main springs using three knots per spring.

2 At the back corners, fold the hessian back and make a cut into the corner. Trim away excess (see page 62).

CALCULATING HESSIAN FOR FRONT RAIL SPRUNG EDGE
To calculate the size of the hessian needed when there is a sprung edge on the front of a chair frame: measure from the top of the back rail over the springs, down into the well formed by the sprung edge, over this edge and onto the front rail. Measure the widest distance from side to side, and add 2.5 cm (1 in) all around for turnings.

3 Release the tacks at the front, and tuck the hessian down into the well between the edge springs and the main springs.

4 Place a piece of string or webbing in the well that is formed, and anchor at either side on the top of the side rail with large tacks. This is known as a well cord. If placed correctly, the cord will sit in the well, tacked at either side on the top of the side rail.

5 Fold the hessian back to reveal the main springs and cut several pieces of cord to act as guy ropes over the well cord. Using a curved needle, take these pieces of twine through the hessian and around the well cord, allowing at least one guy rope between each spring.

6 Secure the end with a slip knot and pull up tight.

7 When all the guy ropes are in place, tack the end of the cord onto the top of the front rail using 16 mm (⅝ in) tacks or staples.

8 Bring the hessian over the sprung edge and tack onto the front of the rail. At the corners, make a neat pleat (as shown, below).

9 Sew the springs on the front edge to the hessian using a blanket stitch and secure the side pleats similarly.

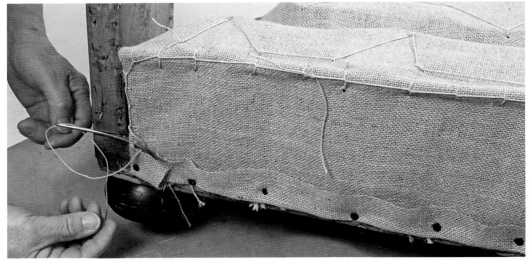

Using hessian elsewhere

Hessian can also be used as a platform for the stuffings on the arms, wings and backs of chairs. Apply it using the same method that has been described for the seats.

Always temporarily tack initially – follow the principle of tacking first on the back, then the front, on the top and bottom, and then side to side. When the hessian is tight, the temporary tacks can be hammered home. Where webbing is used because there is no rail, cut the hessian with a diagonal cut, taking it through the gap between the webbing and the back rail, and then stitch it to the webbing using a running stitch.

Hessian is tacked onto the side rail, and then stitched to a strip of webbing.

The finished effect should look neat and feel durable.

Forming an edge roll

An edge roll, found on the edge of certain types of chairs, replaces a stitched edge and prevents hair being pushed to the back of the seat when it is used. There may be an edge roll at the front, or on the sides as well. On a stool, the edge roll may go the whole way around. An edge roll may also appear around the scroll edge of an arm, or wing, in which case it replaces a stitched edge. An edge roll was often used in Edwardian times to save using expensive hair.

MAKING AN EDGE ROLL

An edge roll can be made with wadding, hair or coir and formed into a roll with hessian. Cut the hessian an extra 10 cm (4 in) larger than the size of the chair where the roll is to go, and tack onto the front rail. Roll pieces of white cotton wadding or handfuls of hair into the excess hessian, and roll up tightly, inserting tacks in the back of the roll, making sure the roll is flush with the front rail. Edge roll can also be bought in foam or paper form, which can then be attached using large tacks, and is used principally around the scroll end of arms and wings.

1 Cut the hessian several centimetres (or inches) longer than is necessary and place a wad of white cotton wadding (or another relevant stuffing) on the top at the edge of the chair.

2 Roll the hessian over the wadding and tuck it underneath to form a tight roll.

3 Insert long tacks at the back of the roll to anchor it down. Fold the corners over the stuffing and tack down neatly.

Use foam tack roll to create a scroll edge around the arm of the chair. This can also be used around a wing, or sometimes on the edge of a seat.

Tools and materials

- **Hair:** For the stuffing

- **Coir, black fibre,** or **wadding:** For the stuffing

- **Scrim:** To cover the hair

- **Springing needle or large curved needle:** For stitching bridle stitches

- **Long double-pointed needle:** For stitching stuffing ties

- **Twine:** For stitching

- **Scissors**

- **Improved tacks 13 mm (½ in)** and **10 mm (⅜ in)**

- **Hammer**

- **Regulator**

- **Rasp:** To create a bevelled edge on the front rail

- **Tape measure**

- **Tailor's chalk**

✳ UPHOLSTERER'S TIP
Always use twine from the centre of the ball to prevent it from unwinding.

Twine

First stuffings

Now that the piece of furniture has a secure base, it's time to think about the stuffing. On a traditional piece, this will be of hair, coir or black fibre, or maybe rubberized hair.

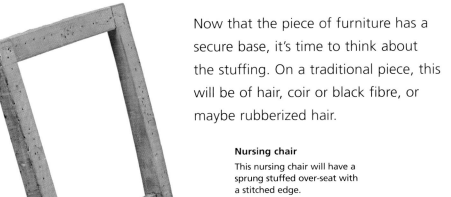

Nursing chair
This nursing chair will have a sprung stuffed over-seat with a stitched edge.

Most chairs have stuffing of some sort. The age and type of chair determines the kind of stuffing used and how much is required. If it's a traditional chair, it may have one or two layers of hair stuffing, followed by a layer of wadding, depending on the chair and whether or not it has springs. When hair is used, it's attached to the chair by bridles, (loops of twine stitched into the hessian).

The amount and thickness of stuffing required is determined by the size of the chair and the finished height. If the chair requires a modern stuffing, then foam or rubberized hair can be used. The latter can sometimes also be used effectively on traditional pieces.

The stuffing on traditional chairs varies according to the type and shape of the piece. Some chairs have only one stuffing, for example a drop-in seat, while others, such as a stuffed over-seat, require at least two stuffings and a stitched edge.

The following section describes how to do the first stuffing on drop-in seats and stuffed over-seats.

Drop-in seat (traditional style)

Drop-in seats only have one layer of stuffing and no stitched edge; as a result, it's best to use real animal hair. They don't need a stitched edge as the frame of the chair supports the stuffed pad (see opposite).

Pincushion seat

A pincushion seat has a single stuffing of hair on top of the hessian and webbing.

When the pad is made of hair, bridles must be stitched onto the hessian (see opposite). Hair can then be stuffed under the bridles to form an even mat, covered with white cotton wadding, and finally, covered with calico.

Sewing bridles

Bridles are loops that are sewn into the hessian to hold the hair in place. Without them, the hair would be piled in an uncontrollable heap on top of the chair. Follow the following steps to make the bridles.

1 Cut a 3 m (10 ft) length of twine, thread the springing needle, and anchor the twine in the back left-hand corner of the hessian.

2 Make a slip knot (see page 49) and pull tightly to the hessian.

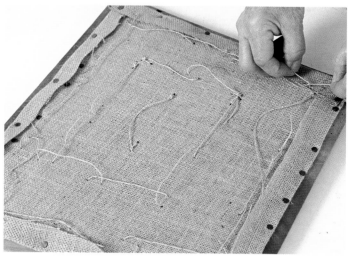

3 Sew four to five overlapping loops across the back of the chair. The loops should be as wide as the palm of your hand and be loose enough for your hand to fit underneath easily. The loops should not be knotted down individually, but left to loosen or tighten according to the hair underneath.

4 The loops can be sewn in rows or in a square shape, as in the picture. The rows should be no more than 7.5 cm (3 in) apart. The twine is finished with a reef knot (see page 55).

Inserting stuffing

Stuff approximately 250 gm (1 lb) of real hair under the
bridles evenly over the seat, making a slight dome shape in
the middle. Then tease the hair out to form an even mat
without holes.

1 Insert a handful of hair under the first loop
that was made, and then do the same under
the second loop and subsequent loops. Make sure
that the hair reaches the edge of the seat frame.

2 If the loops are filled in the order they were
inserted, then each one tightens up the next
one and helps to make the bed of hair even.

3 Continue stuffing the seat until all the loops
are filled with hair, and then tease the hair
together to make a nice flat mat. If there are any
holes in the mat, more hair should be added.

Covering with wadding

Cover the hair on the seat with a layer of white cotton wadding to prevent the
hair from working its way through the covering of calico and final top cover.
Cut the white cotton wadding to size, place it on top of the hair, and then tear
it so that it fits around the edge of the chair.

1 First, measure the area to be covered with wadding to
determine how much is required.

2 Wadding is difficult to cut with scissors and is better torn. Torn edges are also
easier to tease together if a join has to be made. Remove the paper backing from
the wadding and place it on top of the hair. Then tear the surplus away so that it just
covers the hair but does not hang over the wooden frame at the side, as this may
prevent the chair seat from fitting the frame.

Covering with calico

Cover the white cotton wadding with a piece of calico. This should be big enough to completely cover the stuffing and be tacked underneath the frame. The calico is then tightened over the stuffing, relieving the tension from the final top cover.

1 To measure for calico, take a tape measure over the top of the wadding and underneath the frame, adding 5 cm (2 in) extra so that the calico can be held easily in the hand when tensioning.

2 Place the calico on the top of the wadding, making sure that it's on squarely with the grain going straight from back to front and side to side.

- frame
- webbing
- hessian
- hair
- wadding
- calico

> ※ **UPHOLSTERER'S TIP**
> *If you don't have a tape measure on hand, use your forearm as a guide. The distance from the tip of your finger to your elbow measures about 45 cm (18 in), which is the approximate depth of an average chair.*

3 Turn the whole seat over and position the seat and stuffing centrally on the calico.

4 Before tacking down, make sure that the stuffing of hair and white cotton wadding does not overhang the sides of the frame. You should tuck the stuffing in or remove it if there is too much.

5 Pull the calico firmly over the hair and wadding and insert a temporary tack on the underneath of the frame.

6 Insert several more temporary tacks on either side of the original tack, then turn the frame around and do the same on the other three sides.

7 Removing two or three tacks at a time, tighten the calico using one hand to smooth the calico to the back and the other to retack.

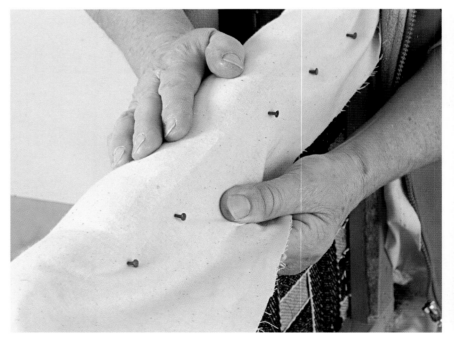

8 When retacking, make sure the stuffing on top of the frame edge is even and with no dips. If there are dips, more hair or wadding should be added underneath the calico.

Anchoring and cutting the corners

Once the calico has been tightened at the sides, you will need to neatly tack down the corners. The pleats formed on the corners should be as flat as possible.

1 Take the calico over one of the back corners of the seat and secure with a tack underneath.

2 Draw a "V" shape either side of the tack to indicate where the cut should be made.

3 Cut up to the "V" shape in a straight line, and then along the line of the "V" making a "Y"-shaped cut.

4 Cut away excess fabric after the "Y" cut has been made to reduce the amount of fabric that will needed to be folded under. Make folds in the calico at the corners, and cut away any excess fabric that is underneath the fold, before tacking it down.

5 Neaten the pleats with the blunt end of a regulator.

6 Tack one pleat down with a small tack. Trim away the fabric beyond the tack and then tack the second pleat, trimming away any excess fabric. Repeat this on all corners.

7 Check that the calico is still tight on the top. Now that it is tacked all around and the corners are finished, the tacks can be hammered home (as seen, left).

Chairs with a stitched edge

Black fibre and coir are better stuffings than real hair for chairs with a stitched edge, as they eventually form a firmer pad and edge roll. However, they must be used generously.

✳ UPHOLSTERER'S TIP
When you are measuring fabric for the seat, remember to add at least 6 cm (2½ in) all around for tucking under.

Because it is softer, hair is often more difficult to form into the firm edge required later on for a stitched edge, but you can use it. Remember that hair from an old chair can be washed and reused (see page 36). The seat illustrated here is a frame that sits on top of a chair frame anchored with a peg at the front (see also page 81).

You will need about 250 gm (1 lb) of stuffing (hair, coir or black fibre) for a dining seat averaging 46 cm (18 in) by 43 cm (17 in). You may have to add more later if necessary. Follow the first stuffing instructions as for the drop-in seat (see page 69–70) for stitching bridles and stuffing with hair. Then follow the instructions below before you stitch the edge.

1 Stitch bridles onto the chair top as previously described (see page 69) and stuff with at least 250 gm (1lb) of hair, coir or black fibre. The hair should be teased into an even mat over the whole surface with no dips or holes.

2 Typically, a piece of scrim measuring around 61 cm (24 in) square is about right for an average dining chair. Lay the scrim over the stuffing.

3 Temporarily tack the scrim down on the outside of the underside of the rails at the back and front, and on both sides.

4 Ensure that the weave of the fabric is straight in both vertical and horizontal directions. Failure to do so will cause later problems.

Stuffing ties

Stuffing ties are stitched through the scrim to the hessian and are used to anchor the scrim in place. Where there are springs, take the stitches through the hessian only and not through the springs and webbing.

1 Using tailor's chalk, draw a square on the scrim about 10 cm (4 in) in from the perimeter of the seat.

2 Take the unthreaded point of the needle right through the scrim and the hessian at the back left-hand corner of the drawn square. Return the needle up through the scrim 2.5 cm (1 in) away.

3 Having pulled the needle completely through the scrim, make a slip knot on top, and tighten.

4 Pass the needle through the scrim once again following the chalk line. Make each stitch length approximately 2.5 cm (1 in).

5 When all the stitches are complete, pull the twine tight and tie with a bow. This allows for adjustment later.

You should continue your stitching all around the marked square, as shown above.

Tacking down the scrim

Now the scrim is stitched in place with stuffing ties, it needs to be tacked to the bevelled edge of the frame.

✳ UPHOLSTERER'S TIP
It is difficult to tack into a corner, so bevel the edge with a rasp.

1 Remove the tacks from underneath the chair frame and add extra hair to the stuffing to ensure that the rolled edge is filled generously, but evenly.

2 Tuck the scrim underneath the hair to form a round edge that is full of hair. (The scrim can be trimmed at this stage if there is too much to tuck under.)

3 Tension the scrim to form a firm edge before tacking it down.

4 Tack the scrim onto the edge using 10 mm (⅜ in) tacks. Start in the centre of the chair frame and move outwards.

5 Keep adding tacks along the front edge, putting the tacks in temporarily, and working to within 5 cm (2 in) of the corners. Repeat this process on the back and sides, trimming the scrim if there's too much to tuck under.

Front and back corners

Once you have tacked the scrim around the chair, it's time to finish the corners. Make a neat square pleat at the front. The type of pleat you make at the back depends on the type of chair you're using and the corner's finish.

Front corners

1 Tack to the end of the side rail. Bring a side piece of scrim around the corner to the front and make a small cut 2.5 cm (1 in) from the corner.

2 Unfold the fabric, and cut a square of fabric using the cut already made as a guide.

3 You may find you have to add more hair under the scrim on the corner. It is much easier to pleat the fabric around hair than air!

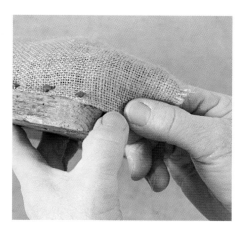

4 Tack the scrim to the edge at the front corner. Now take the fabric round to the side ready to make a pleat.

5 Make a front-facing pleat with the excess fabric. Ensure that the pleat lies on the straight weave.

6 Trim away the excess fabric, tuck underneath, and tack down onto the chair rail.

7 Using the blunt end of a regulator, neatly tuck the scrim underneath the hair, making sure there are no wisps of hair showing.

8 Before tacking the edge, use the regulator to make sure the hair underneath the scrim is evenly distributed.

9 Secure the pleat of the scrim by putting a tack in the corner. Also, anchor the side of the pleat with a tack and hammer home.

Unusual back corners

1 Some seat frames have the corner cut out and will need to be treated in a different way. Start at the back corners and begin by folding the scrim back.

2 Make sure there is plenty of hair in the corner for the scrim to go around and if more hair is needed, pack it in well using your thumb.

3 Make a diagonal cut in the scrim just up to the cut out corner.

4 Fold the fabric underneath, and place a tack in the corner of the top of the frame.

5 Having cut away any excess scrim, use the blunt end of the regulator to help tuck the fabric underneath into a neat pleat.

6 Repeat this on the other side of the corner using the regulator to neaten the fold.

7 After tucking down on both sides of the corner, tack down neatly on the top of the rail.

Checking tension

Once the seat has been temporarily tacked all around, check the tension of the scrim. If the tension is even, hammer home the tacks. The stuffed seat should have a firm, vertical rounded edge – not too tight, nor too loose.

Now that the tacks are all hammered home, use a regulator to move the hair underneath the scrim, as shown above and right. This ensures that the pad is neat and even. The seat is now ready for the edge roll to be stitched (see over the page).

Regulator

Stitching an edge

A stitched edge is formed by one or more rows of blind stitching followed by an edge roll. Blind stitching is so called because the stitches are visible from the side of the chair but not the top.

Tools and materials

- **A double-pointed needle:** Use a 20 cm (8 in) or 25 cm (10 in) depending on the size of the seat.

- **Regulator:** To regulate the hair.

- **Good quality twine:** Barbour No. 3 or No. 4.

- **Scissors**

- **Glove**

- **Highlighter**

- **Tailor's chalk**

Double-pointed needles

The aim of this technique is to build up a firm edge on a chair that will keep its shape when sat on. It can also be applied to arms, wings and the top of backs of chairs – in fact any place where a firm edge is required.

It is usual for two rows of stitching to be applied to a dining chair, but an armchair or large sofa with a deep seat will require three or four rows.

Highlighter

Tailor's chalk

The aim is to create a firm edge of hair so that when the seat has been used for some time, the stuffing remains in place and does not go out of shape. You should end up with a solid edge roll, straight side and square corners, as seen here.

❋ **UPHOLSTERER'S TIP**
When using twine, to ensure that you pull it as tight as possible, wear a glove to prevent the twine from cutting into your palm.

Starting to blind stitch

The process starts with a slip knot. First, thread your needle with about 3 m (10 ft) of twine. Always use this amount as 2 m (6½ ft) will never be enough and 4 m (13 ft) will fray before you reach the end. If you are right-handed, then work from left to right. Reverse this if left-handed.

Take care when taking the needle and thread through the hessian – do not take it through the springs, if there are any. Similarly, don't take the needle and twine right out of the scrim to form a stitch on the top, as this will impede the tightening of the hair. The twine should go around the hair between the hessian and scrim and pull towards the edge – if you can visualize this, it becomes more obvious why a stitched edge is necessary.

1 With the left hand side of the chair facing you, take the unthreaded end of the needle and insert it into the scrim close to the back corner. Scrape the edge of the rail as you do so.

2 Pull the needle through the scrim, and bring it out near to the stuffing ties so that the eye of the needle can be seen.

Bring the needle through the scrim so that the eye can be seen.

3 Return the needle back through the scrim, about 2.5 cm (1 in) from the chair leg.

4 Once you have pulled the needle and twine through, place the needle in a safe place on top of the chair with the sharp point facing away from you, and tie the twine with a slip knot (see page 49).

First row of blind stitching

Blind stitches can be seen from the side of the chair, but not from the top. A different chair is used here.

✳ Upholsterer's Tip
Always use Coats Barbour twine, usually No. 3 or No. 4, and never cheap twine which is weak and flawed. Nylon twine isn't suitable either because it's not a natural yarn and has a tendency to slip when stitched.

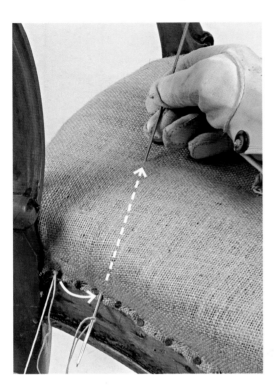

1 Keep the twine from the slip knot on the left, and insert the unthreaded end of the needle into the scrim about 5 cm (2 in) along to the right. Pull the needle out close to the stuffing ties in the centre of the chair, but only until you can see the eye and no further.

2 Return the needle back through the scrim to where the slip knot is making a wide "V" shape underneath the scrim, brushing the frame of the wood as the needle is brought through.

3 Wind the left twine around the needle three times, and pull the needle through. As a safety measure, put the needle in the top of the chair, pointing away from the body.

4 Taking care not to break the twine, pull the knot that has formed towards you tightly to the right, so that the knot slides along.

If the stitch has been made correctly, with the twine from the left being wound round the needle three times, the knot will slide along (as seen here) as opposed to remaining in a tight knot.

5 This stitch should not be in a tight knot, but travel along. Work the stitch around the chair, including the back if possible.

Take care at the corners so that they are not flattened but kept square (as seen, right). A short stitch on the corner is useful. Think about what the twine is doing under the scrim – it should be pulling the hair towards the edge in a fat wedge, not a thin one.

6 Once you have reached the end of a row make a short stitch and then wind the twine in your left hand around the needle, followed by the twine in your right hand. Pull the twine through to form a knot. Avoid taking the twine around the inside of a chair leg – it is always better to finish off at the end of a row and start again with a slip knot.

Joining twine with a reef knot
Since a granny knot will come undone when pulled, join twine using a reef knot (see page 55). Make the knot close to where the twine has been pulled through on the chair. It's not possible to take the knot through the scrim when sewing.

Second row of blind stitching

On a stuffed over-seat, a second row of blind stitching is necessary to build up the stitched edge. In this row, the stitch is the same as in the first row, but the needle and twine emerge halfway between the stuffing ties and the chair edge. This moves the hair closer to the edge.

1 Make a second row 13 mm (½ in) above the previous row. To stitch accurately, mark it on the scrim with a highlighter or tailor's chalk.

2 Start with a slip knot – as with the first row of stitching. Now, take the needle into the scrim on the marked line to emerge from the top of the scrim – about halfway between the edge of the chair and the stuffing ties.

3 The stitch should be repeated all round the chair as with the first row.

Edge Roll

Now that there's a firm amount of hair at the edge, it's ready for the final roll. Adjustments can be made with the regulator to ensure the even distribution of the hair along the edge, and to prevent it from being soft or lumpy.

1 Mark a line on the side of the scrim 6 mm (¼ in) above the last row of blind stitching. Now make another line on the top of the scrim approximately 2.5 cm (1 in) from the edge of the top surface, taking the inside corner of the back leg as a guide.

2.5 cm (1 in)

1.3 cm (½ in)

2 Starting with a slip knot, take the needle through the scrim and out completely on the top, then return through the fabric about 5 cm (2 in) back. Pull through.

3 Wind the twine around the needle three times, and pull the needle through to complete the stitch. Aim to get as much hair as possible into the roll to make it firm.

4 Make sure the side of the stitched edge is vertical, and not sloping in or out. Beginners may find this procedure difficult, but practice will help you improve. When going around a scroll edge on an arm, one row will be enough. The stitching is now complete.

A regulator (right) is used to gather the hairs at the edge of the chair so that the roll is full.

Some variations

For chairs that have some show wood around the area where the roll needs to be, for example, on the inside back of a chair, use a large curved needle instead of the double-pointed straight one. Then only one row of blind stitching is usually needed, plus the edge roll.

When stitching an edge around the scroll end of an arm or wing, it's usual to have only one row of blind stitching followed by the roll edge (as seen, right).

Tools and materials

- **Twine:** for bridles

- **Hair:** Approx 250 gm (1 lb) per small chair

- **White cotton wadding or cotton wadding:** to cover the hair

- **Calico:** to cover the wadding

- **Curved needle**

- **Magnetic hammer**

- **10 mm (⅜ in) fine tacks**

- **Scissors**

- **Tape measure**

- **Pencil for marking**

Curved needle

❋ UPHOLSTERER'S TIP
The upholstery process is identical for both sofas and chairs: a sofa just needs larger pieces of fabric and more stuffing. The order of upholstering a large chair is normally: back, arms, wings, and finally, the seat.

Second stuffings

Now you have finished the first stuffing and stitched edge, your chair will have taken on a new shape. Gone is the nice rounded finish and in its place is a rather uncomfortable looking seat, with a firm edge and a hollow middle. A second stuffing is required to make the chair comfortable again.

The hair that once covered the chair has been pulled to the side, and now the second stuffing will fill this space to recreate the rounded shape that was previously there. Once the second stuffing of hair has been positioned, cover with thick cotton wadding, and then calico. The white cotton wadding prevents the hairs creeping through the calico and top fabric, which would be uncomfortable to sit on. The use of calico enables the stuffing to be tightened before the top fabric is put on. This also means that if the top fabric ever needs to be replaced, then the stuffing will stay in place. Follow the steps below to make this second stuffing.

Attaching bridles

With the stitched edge completed, more bridles need to be stitched to the scrim. Follow the instructions for these as you did in the first stuffing (see page 68). Bridles stitched on a larger piece should be 10 cm (4 in) in length and in rows that are 10 cm (4 in) apart. The stitches should reach the extremity of the seat, both in width and length. Backs and arms require the same process. Using a curved springing needle and twine make loops on the scrim to anchor the hair.

Stuffing hair

Stuff the bridles with real hair, or washed old hair – as long as the hair hasn't disintegrated into small pieces.

※ UPHOLSTERER'S TIP
*Useful measurements:
The length of your forearm, from fingertip to elbow, is approximately 45 cm (18 in)
The length from your thumb to your first joint is approximately 2.5 cm (1 in) The span of your palm, from little finger to thumb is approximately 20 cm (8 in).*

1 Take handfuls of the hair and tuck it under the bridles, starting at the back and following the bridles in the order that they were stitched in. When this has been done all over the seat, back or arm, tease the hair out so that it forms a thick mat with no dents or holes.

2 Where the hair has gone thin under the scrim with the first stuffing, make sure the area is well covered with the second stuffing. The whole stuffing should be 5 to 7.6 cm (2 to 3 in) deep, depending on the size of the chair. If you are reusing hair, make sure that it's well teased out and not in tight knots.

Covering with white cotton wadding

The next step is to cover the hair with white cotton wadding, which comes in two thicknesses. The thinner wadding – which is 28 gm (2½ oz) – is usually thick enough. This prevents the hair working its way through the calico and top fabric. Measure from the back of the seat to the front, and tear off a piece of white cotton wadding the same size – it's better torn, as it is difficult to cut with scissors.

1 Remove the paper or backing from the wadding and place on top of the hair.

2 Tear the white cotton wadding so it hangs just over the side of the chair roll. If the roll isn't exactly vertical, place a piece of wadding along the side edge to recreate a straight edge.

Anchoring calico

Use calico to cover the white cotton wadding and anchor down all the stuffings.

1 Measure the length of the seat from the bottom of the back rail, over the stuffing, down to the bottom of the front rail, and across the middle to the sides. Allow an extra 5 cm (2 in) of material to tack down.

2 Place the calico on top of the wadding and anchor first at the front, then at the back with temporary tacks into the single thickness of fabric. The calico does not need to be turned under.

3 Continue this temporary tacking at the side edges of the chair, gradually working from the centre to the corners.

4 Make cuts at the back corner, by folding the calico back into a "V" shape and cutting into the corner, as with the hessian and scrim.

5 The ears of fabric produced by the first cut can then be removed leaving 2.5 cm (1 in) to tuck under.

Pleating

It's now time to pleat the front corners. This can be done as a straight pleat when the top of the leg of the chair is square shaped or with two pleats making a tulip shape when the chair leg has a curved or shaped corner.

1 Tack the calico to the end of the side rails, bring it to the front, and pull it down slightly. Tack the calico onto the front rail, just around the corner, and make a fold in the material.

2 Cut away any excess that's in the fold, which generally takes the form of a square shape. A cut edge always sits better than a fold.

3 Tuck in the excess fabric and make a pleat in the calico, using the straight grain of the fabric on the edge of the pleat. Use the blunt end of the regulator to make the pleat sit straight. This pleat can then be tacked down.

Tulip pleat

A tulip pleat is best suited to a chair with curved corners. It has a double pleat which will hug the edge of the show wood neatly.

1 Pull calico over the front corner of the chair leg and anchor with a tack.

2 A pleat should be made either side of the centre tack, using the blunt end of the regulator to neaten the pleat. Both of these pleats can then be tacked down. (See page 95 for a finished tulip pleat.)

※ UPHOLSTERER'S TIP
Calico that has been treated with a fire retardant is often brittle, so be careful that it doesn't tear at the cut corners. Often, using untreated calico and a fire retardant barrier cloth is a better idea.

Tightening calico

The calico needs to be taut. To achieve this, either sit on the chair, or put a weighty object on it for 24 hours. Then, smooth the top of the calico with your left hand, pull it down with the right, and tack down with temporary tacks on the side of the rails before permanently tacking.

1 Remove the temporary tacks one at a time and retack after tightening down as shown in Step 2. If any holes in the hair can be seen through the calico then the calico will have to be removed and more hair added under the wadding.

2 After removing the temporary tacks, tighten the calico using your hand to smooth the fabric from the top to the sides.

3 Once you are satisfied that the seat is firm and nicely rounded, hammer the tacks home and trim the calico close to the tack line. Make sure the line of tacks is not too close to the show wood, if there is any, because the calico will be seen when the top cover is attached.

Applying calico to the seat of large armchairs

Marking and cutting the back corners of the calico on large chairs is often difficult. You will need to push the calico through from the front, and tack it down at the back.

1 Measure the gap between the inside back legs. In this example it is approximately 51 cm (20 in).

2 Measure from the inside corner to the bottom of the back rail. In this example it is 12.5 cm (5 in).

12.5 cm (5 in)

raw edge

25 cm (10 in)

folded edge

3 Measure the chair at the widest point – from back to front and left to right. Cut a piece of calico, adding 7.5 cm (3 in) all round for the turnings. With the calico folded in half lengthways make a mark 25 cm (10 in) from the fold and 12.5 cm (5 in) from the raw edge. Cut diagonally towards this mark to form a wedge shape. Push this shape through from the front of the seat to the back and tack down on the outside of the back seat rail.

Applying calico round a flat rail or flat curved arm

When cutting calico – and subsequently the top fabric – round a flat rail, it is important to mark the exact point at which the fabric goes round the rail. This is best done with a pen or pencil and tape measure.

1 With the calico attached with temporary tacks at the front and back of the chair fold the calico back at the side and mark the rear edge of the rail with a pencil.

2 Measure the length of the rail with a tape measure.

3 Transfer this measurement to the calico with this tape, using the first mark as a starting point.

4 Make an angled "Y" cut to these marks.

Where the rail is wide and it is difficult to tuck in the calico tightly, stitch a length of twine through the calico, taking the needle and twine through the webbing to the underside of the chair and fix with a tack (as seen, right).

5 The calico can then be pulled down on either side of the arm support and tacked onto the outside of the chair rail. Trim the excess calico close to the line of tacks.

Tools and materials

- **Item of furniture:** to measure for re-covering

- **Notepad and pencil**

- **Soft tape measure**

- **metre or yard rule**

- **Cutting table**

- **Tailor's chalk**

- **Sharp scissors**

※ UPHOLSTERER'S TIP
On a chair seat the pile of the fabric has to come from back to front so that when you stand up from the chair, the fabric pile follows.

Planning your fabric cuts

Once you have chosen a piece of furniture to upholster, you'll need to decide on the top cover and how much material is needed to make it. The first step is to take measurements of the necessary components and draw up a cutting plan to estimate the correct quantity of fabric. A chair is used for the cutting plan in this example.

Take measurements from the chair either before it is stripped or after the new upholstery has been completed. If the chair has been stripped to the frame, measure the fabric generously. Use the old pieces of fabric as a pattern, but again, measure generously to allow for new padding and turnings. Always cut the fabric pieces into squares or rectangles, and mark the underside so you know what piece it is and which side is the top.

Most upholstery fabric is 1.35 m (54 in) wide, but it is occasionally wider, so check before you start the plan. Fabric with a directional pattern will go from top to bottom on the back and from back to front on the seat. This also applies to fabric with a pile, such as velvet. With this type of fabric the warp yarns go vertically and the weft yarns horizontally or parallel to the floor on the seat.

Drawing up the plan

Sketch out a chart to note the name of the fabric component, the number it requires, the abbreviation it uses, and its length and width. These measurements can then be transferred to the cutting plan.

1 Draw a chart for the measurements of the components and an outline of a cutting plan, as shown in the diagram.

2 Take accurate measurements of the chair's components with a tape measure and record them on the chart. Measure the largest pieces first – the seat, and then the inside back, measuring first the length, followed by the width. The covers for inside arms, outside arms and cushions can usually be taken from half the width. The pieces for the wings and facings can usually be taken from the offcuts.

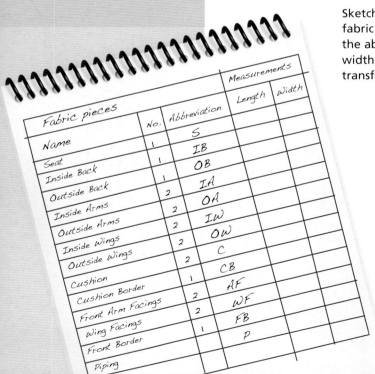

Fabric pieces			Measurements	
Name	No.	Abbreviation	Length	Width
Seat	1	S		
Inside Back	1	IB		
Outside Back	1	OB		
Inside Arms	2	IA		
Outside Arms	2	OA		
Inside Wings	2	IW		
Outside Wings	2	OW		
Cushion	2	C		
Cushion Border	1	CB		
Front Arm Facings	2	AF		
Wing Facings	2	WF		
Front Border	1	FB		
Piping		P		

Railroaded fabrics

Sometimes, a pattern is woven along the length (fig 2) rather than across the width (fig 1). This is known as railroaded fabric, which is excellent for large settees and chaises, especially ones that require a fabric width that is larger than the standard length – that is: 1.37 m (54 in).

1

2

3 Transfer the measurements to the cutting plan. Note the different plans for plain and patterned fabrics. Once you've recorded the measurements on the plan, total up the length measurements to figure the amount of fabric you'll need.

4 Spread the fabric out on a large table or a tabletop on trestles and mark the required pieces, either with tailor's chalk or pins, using the cutting plans illustrated as a guide. A metre or yard rule is useful here for marking straight lines. Using sharp scissors, cut the fabric into the various components, marking each one on the back with its name (use the abbreviations suggested on page 35).

Checklist

1. Before you start marking and cutting the fabric, ask yourself the following questions: Is this the correct fabric? Is it the correct length and width? Is it the correct colour? Is it dirty or damaged? Are there any flaws in the yardage? Have I forgotten anything, such as seam allowances?

2. Check the size of your workbench: this should ideally be large enough to lay out the required pieces for patterning.

3. Make sure you have all your tools close at hand: chalk, masking tape (or pieces of paper for labelling), pins and sharp scissors.

4. Check the pattern: does it need to be centred on the furniture? Is it correctly placed on the yardage to be cut? If there are stripes, are they aligned? Have you taken into account the seams that might appear in the wrong place (the middle of the inside back, for example)? When you have the patterns in place, remember you need to allow for seams – do not forget to include this in your figures for the original measuring.

5. Now mark and cut all pieces for the furniture. Label the pieces with masking tape or paper and stick the labels onto each piece of fabric. Don't forget to mark the direction of the top and bottom on the fabric. If your workspace is limited, cut the large pieces first, and the pieces you will need to attach first.

Tips for taking the correct measurements

Make sure that when you measure for a new cover you do it carefully and accurately. Allow enough fabric for the seams if you are sewing pieces together, extra fabric for tucking in, and extra fabric to hold onto when attaching it to the frame. It is unwise to use the existing fabric to make new patterns, except for the cushions and front facings. Make sure you cut the main pieces into squares and rectangles so you can adjust the fabric to the frame and new padding.

First, take the measurements for the largest pieces – the length is for those pieces that will run up the roll, the width is for those pieces running across the covering fabric. Do not include the selvedge (uncut edge) of the fabric in your measuring and cutting. In traditional upholstery, a measured estimate is usually good enough. Slightly oversized pieces are fine, as any trimming or shaping takes place during the upholstery and hand finishing afterwards.

Tools and materials

- **Fabric**

- **Black base fabric:** for covering the bottom of the chair to act as a barrier cloth (see page 113)

- **Magnetic hammer**

- **Staple gun (optional) and staples**

- **10 mm (⅜ in) fine tacks**

- **Tack remover**

- **Tape measure**

- **Sharp scissors**

- **Pins**

- **Regulator**

- **Marker pen**

Tack remover

Tacks

Attaching new coverings

Now you can begin the exciting top cover stage. Whether you're covering a simple dining chair or a more complicated piece like a wing chair, the method you'll use to attach the fabric remains the same. A dining chair is used as the example in this article.

Use care and consideration when you choose upholstery fabric. Strong fabric is needed for a chair with heavy use, and lighter fabric for an occasional chair. The type of fabric also depends on the style of the chair. Some people feel that an antique chair should be covered in an imitation of the original fabric, while others choose something entirely new. Once you have chosen the fabric (see pages 24–29), you will need to cut it out (see drawing up a cutting plan on pages 92–93).

Covering a balloon-backed chair with a patterned fabric

Measure the chair, cut the fabric accordingly, and arrange the material centrally to accentuate the pattern. Mark the centre-back and centre-front with a pin or tailor's tack.

⁂ **Upholsterer's Tip**
It's always a good idea to temporarily tack first so you can easily make adjustments. Ensure the width of the braid or gimp that covers the cut raw edge of the fabric also covers the line of tacks.

1 Mark the centre of the fabric and the centre of the chair frame with a marker pen. Align the two marks to ensure the fabric is straight. Repeat on the back of the chair.

2 Attach the centre of the fabric with three tacks at the front, back and sides so that the weave of the fabric is straight on the chair from back to front and side to side.

3 Fold the fabric at the corners back and cut to the inside corner.

When you pull the fabric down into the corner of the leg of the chair it should sit tight and neat (as seen above).

4 Open up the cut and pull the fabric to either side of the leg.

5 Fold the excess fabric back and cut off the ears at the side and the back.

6 Fold the excess fabric underneath. Check that the fold is on the straight grain of the fabric and tack down. If the fold is on the cross grain, it won't sit straight. Repeat on the other back corner.

7 This chair has a rounded edge at the front corners so a double or tulip pleat is required. Take the fabric over the corner and tack down.

8 The pleats should meet at the edge of the show wood. Use the blunt end of the regulator for perfecting the crease of the pleat and make sure that the gimp or braid (see pages 112–113) will cover both the tacks and the raw edge when it is applied.

The straight back rail

In this sequence you will learn how to attach fabric to chairs with straight rails, sloping side rails, square front legs and straight back legs. You must make a "Y" cut in the fabric to go round straight rails and insert a small piece of fabric in the gap created at the side.

1 Mark the fabric as for the scrim on page 75 and make a "Y" cut to take the fabric round the rail. Choose a small piece of fabric 5 cm (2 in) longer and 7.5 cm (3 in) wider than the gap, making sure that the pattern and direction of the pile go in the same direction as the fabric at the back of the seat. Take a strip of back tacking or narrow card the width of the back rail and tack through the card and fabric.

2 Pull the fabric down over the gap and tack underneath the seat frame.

3 Fold the seat fabric over the raw edges of the insert and tack underneath. Any fullness at the back of the chair is taken up with one or two pleats.

The sloping side rail

It's awkward to make the cut on a side rail and easy to cut in the wrong place so take care and work slowly.

1 Fold the fabric back and mark the rear cutting point with a pin. Note that this mark will be further forward than you expect.

2 Create a second mark with a pin and make a "Y" cut to these marks. Never cut right up to the mark; further cutting can be done if necessary but a cut cannot be rejoined.

If the fabric has a small amount of stretch and the cut has been made correctly, then you will be able to pull the fabric round and fold it over without inserting an extra fabric piece (as seen above).

Square front legs

Square front legs with show wood on the corner require
several cuts and a straight pleat to make a neat corner.

1 Fold the fabric back and make a diagonal cut to the corner of the leg. Trim off excess.

2 Make a similar cut at the top of the leg. Trim off the excess, leaving enough to fold under and around the top of the leg. Use a regulator for this.

3 Take the folded fabric around the corner, pulling it down slightly. Anchor with a tack. Make a diagonal cut in the fold underneath.

4 Cut out the excess fabric underneath the fold. Cut out a square shape and make another diagonal cut into the top corner of the show wood.

5 Fold the fabric underneath, form a neat pleat on the corner and tack home. This can be anchored permanently with either a tack, gimp pin or decorative nail.

Straight back legs

Pull the top fabric down, mark either side of the chair leg, and cut.

1 Pull the fabric down to the leg. Mark either side of the leg and make a "Y" cut to the marks.

2 Fold the fabric on either side of the leg, making pleats where necessary. Tack underneath, and hammer the tacks home. Only those at the front, above the show wood, will need to be covered with gimp or braid.

Deep buttoning

Tools and materials

- **Hair**

- **Finishing fabric**

- **Calico:** to cover the hair

- **White cotton wadding**

- **Polyester wadding** (medium weight): to protect the white cotton wadding

- **25 cm (10 in) double pointed needle**

- **Nylon twine**

- **Scraps of calico/webbing or hessian:** to act as butterflies behind the knots

- **Slipping thread:** for stitching the calico

- **Regulator**

- **Skewers:** to indicate button marks

- **Pins, covered buttons, tape measure and ruler**

Hair

※ Upholsterer's Tip
Professional upholsterers have buttoning machines to make secure, covered buttons. Kits for making buttons can be bought at fabric shops, but the buttons often come apart when they are tied down.

Deep buttoning on upholstery was introduced in the nineteenth century to add opulence – although not necessarily comfort – to seats. It is widely seen on the backs and arms, rather than seats, of traditionally upholstered chairs and requires the skill of an experienced upholsterer. Deep buttoning is also found on modern chairs and headboards where the use of foam makes it a much easier task.

The stuffing underneath the deep buttoning was traditionally a firm pad of hair, which has been replaced in modern chairs with foam and rubberized hair. It is important to set out and mark the positions of the buttons carefully. Make sure you mark up the fabric accurately so the pleats formed between the buttons lie flat and are of a uniform size. Usually, the buttoning has a diamond pattern where the length is greater than the width. Different shaped patterns should be left until you have mastered the diamond shape. The following instructions are for real hair.

1 Decide on your buttoning pattern and mark the hessian base accordingly using skewers. The type of pattern you use will depend on the size of the space available for buttoning and the style of the chair. As a guide, a diamond shape 12.5 cm (5 in) wide by 17.5 cm (7 in) long is a good size to work from, but it can be smaller or larger. For comfort, and a pleasing appearance, place the bottom row of buttons slightly above the timber area, and in line with the top of the arm. Once the position has been decided, replace the skewer mark with a chalk or pen mark on the back and front of the hessian.

Chair back measurement

11.5 cm
(4.5 in)   12.5 cm
(5 in)   12.5 cm
(5 in)   11.5 cm
(4.5 in)

11.5 cm
(4.5 in)

17.5 cm
(7 in)

25.5 cm
(10 in)

Calico measurement

15 cm
(6 in)   16 cm
(6.5 in)   16 cm
(6.5 in)   15 cm
(6 in)

15 cm
(6 in)

21.5cm
(8.5 in)

29.5 cm
(11.5 in)

5 cm
(2 in) (seam
allowance)

2 Cut a piece of calico large enough to completely cover the buttoned area. Allow an extra 3.75 cm (1½ in) between all the buttons, and from the buttons to the edge. Also allow for a 5 cm (2 in) seam allowance all around. On a chair back, the extra calico goes between the bottom rails and is attached on the outside of this rail. Draw centre lines on the straight grain of the calico to establish the centre of the fabric. Then mark up the calico, allowing an extra 3.75 cm (1½ in) between the button marks. For example, a diamond shape 12.5 cm (5 in) by 17.5 cm (7 in) will become 16.25 cm (6½ in), by 21.25 cm (8½ in). Make sure the markings on the calico are on the straight grain of the fabric, and that enough fabric is left at the top and bottom to be tacked down at the edges.

A small piece of calico (called a butterfly) is inserted under the twine to prevent the twine tearing the calico.

Place a butterfly of hessian or webbing under the slip knot at the back of the chair before pulling it tight.

3 Thread a double-pointed needle with nylon twine. Line up a button mark on the calico with a mark on the hessian. Take the threaded end of the needle through the calico and hessian, about 1.25 cm (½ in) to one side of the mark. Unthread the needle at the back leaving one of the ends of the twine at the back of the hessian. Repeat this with the end of the twine at the front, but 1.25 cm (½ in) from the mark in the opposite direction so that the twine is through the calico and hessian either side of the mark. Place a butterfly under the twine at the front to prevent the twine tearing the calico.

4 Tie a slip knot at the back of the hessian, place a butterfly under the knot and pull it tight. Repeat this with two horizontal rows of button marks. Pockets should now be forming in the calico.

5 Stuff the pockets with plenty of hair. Real hair is softer and easier to use for this than coir or black fibre. This stuffing should be even, with the resulting pleats sitting on top of the hair rather than in a hollow. Large quantities of hair are needed to fill the pockets evenly. Add more hair by pushing it underneath the hair that is already there, rather than over the top. This makes a better shape around the button. The calico can be anchored temporarily at the edges with skewers.

6 A regulator may be used to move the hair into awkward corners and to perfect the pleats. Repeat this process with all the other buttons until the stuffing between the buttons is complete. Secure the slip knots at the back with a reef knot.

✳ UPHOLSTERER'S TIP
The pleats should always face downwards on the back of a chair and forwards on a seat.

7 Now you will fix the calico. Make sure the grain of the fabric is straight, and then make vertical and horizontal pleats from the button nearest to the frame edge. Secure with a skewer. You may have to add more hair to give a round finish to this edge. Smooth the fabric so that there is no fullness or gathering fabric between these pleats. Incorporate any surplus fabric into the pleats.

8 When the buttons are tied down correctly and the stuffing is even and taut, then fix it permanently with tacks; or stitch it to the scrim. Stitching is often easier – use a slip stitch and nylon thread.

❋ UPHOLSTERER'S TIP
When using patterned material think about where the pattern should lie – it can be in the centre or positioned randomly. Buttons can be made into different sizes, although the most common size is 13 mm (½ in).

9 Cover the whole area with white cotton wadding and then polyester wadding. Make large holes in both layers, to indicate where the buttons will sit. The polyester can form a tight ring on the top cover if the holes are not large enough. The chair is now ready for the top cover.

10 Cut a piece of fabric the same size as the calico. If it has a pattern then position it to be in the correct place on the chair when it is buttoned. Mark the button positions on the fabric with pins, making the same allowance for the buttons as on the calico. Do not use chalk or a marker pen here, as the mark will show if you need to alter the button's position. Thread the double-pointed needle with 45.5 cm (18 in) nylon twine, and take the twine from the front through the top fabric, to the left of the pin.

11 Remove the pin from the button mark and take the needle through the hole in the polyester, white cotton wadding and calico to the back of the hessian, going to one side of the butterfly. Remove the twine from the needle leaving an end at the back of the hessian. At the front, thread the other end of the twine through the button. Now rethread the needle and take it through the fabric and stuffing to the back of the chair, passing the other side of the butterfly.

12 Make a slip knot and pull tight as you did previously with the calico. Ensure that the button is sitting flat in the hole. When repeating this with the other buttons, test the position of the mark by placing your finger on it, pushing it into the hole, and then marking it with a skewer. Ensure the fabric between the buttons is taut and on the straight grain. Repeat this process on the arm. If there are no holes in the frame for the button twine to be taken through then pull it through on either side of the frame and anchor with a tack.

If a neat pleat forms diagonally between the buttons, then tie in the second button. Repeat this on the next button to form a diamond pattern (as seen, right). If the fabric has been marked correctly on the straight grain then the pleats will lie flat. When tightening the buttons, make sure the pleats are all folding down, this prevents dust gathering in them.

13 After tightening the buttons at the back, trim the wadding at the front so it will be clear of the tacking down of the top fabric. Now, temporarily tack the top fabric to the frame using 10 mm (⅜ in) tacks. Tack the spaces between the pleats first and then form the remaining fabric into a pleat.

A staple gun with a nozzle (as seen on the left) instead of a flat bed, is ideal for anchoring the top fabric.

Tools required

- **Fabric**
- **Nylon twine**
- **Marking pen**
- **Ruler**
- **Scissors**

Marking Pens

Vandyking

In the context of upholstery, vandyking means to join two pieces of fabric in deep buttoning, without the need for a straight seam. It is most often found on large pieces such as Chesterfields and headboards.

Mark the position of the buttons carefully and accurately on the fabric (see page 98–102) and draw diagonal lines between each button, while keeping the pattern and direction of the pile of the fabric in mind.

1 Draw an extra cutting line 12 mm (½ in) from the edge of the line of buttons to be joined on both pieces of fabric and cut away the excess in a zigzag line.

2 When the excess has been cut away in a zigzag line on both pieces to be joined, they should mirror each other as shown.

3 Pin or tack these two pieces together and machine stitch along the drawn line making sure that the button marks are together.

4 Cut nicks into the seam so that it will stretch over the padding when the buttons are inserted.

5 This simple method of joining will result in an invisible seam when deep buttoned. Here it is viewed from underneath.

Tools and materials for shallow buttoning

- **Buttons**: use a button covering service or a buttoning machine as for deep buttoning.

- **Double-pointed needle**

- **Nylon twine**

- **Scraps of hessian for butterflies**

- **Skewers**

- **Pins**

Double-pointed needles

Shallow buttoning

Shallow buttons sit on the surface of the top fabric rather than in a deep cut hole. They are used for decoration and for taking up slack material on chairs with curved backs.

Shallow buttoning on a chair takes place after the top fabric has been applied and before the outside cover has been attached. Shallow buttons are often used on modern chairs to anchor two pieces of fabric together. They're also applied to the tops and bottoms of cushions to help stabilize them. String is tied underneath the buttons with a reef knot.

Applying shallow buttons to a cushion

Shallow buttons are used on the back and front of this cushion. For the back of a chair, wind twine around a piece of fabric called a "butterfly" and tie securely.

1 Mark the positions of the buttons with pins or skewers on the top and bottom of the fabric. They can be arranged in a square, as shown below, or in a variety of other symmetrical patterns.

2 Pass the threaded end of the needle through the pin mark on the cushion.

These three layouts (above) show alternative button positioning. The button patterns are flexible according to individual requirements.

3 Now, take the needle further, through the mark on the back of the cushion, but only until the eye of the needle can be seen.

❋ Upholsterer's Tip
Place the shank of the button in the hole. This prevents it from wobbling on top of the fabric.

4 With the needle still in the cushion, remove one end of the twine from the needle. Pass this end of the twine through the button shank, rethread the needle and pull the twine through to the back.

5 Unthread the needle and pull the threads so the shank of the button on the reverse side sits in the hole made by the twine.

6 Tie the ends of the twine together with a reef knot and tighten.

7 Secure the knot underneath the button.

8 Pull the knot tight and add another one.

9 Cut the ends very short so that the button can sink into the hole.

Tie shallow buttons that are seen only on one side of the chair or cushion, at the back. Knot the twine round a piece of fabric known as a butterfly to prevent the knot pulling through to the front (as seen, right).

10 Repeat the steps with all the buttons and secure them evenly.

Tools and materials

- **Sewing machine** with a zip foot and double-piping foot.

- **Ruler and Pencil**

- **Rotary cutter or scissors**

- **Piping cord, single and/or double**

- **Fabric**

Rotary cutter

Making single and double piping

Single piping is used to decorate or disguise seams on upholstered chairs. It can be made of the same fabric used on the chair, or a contrasting one. Sew the piping onto the fabric or attach to the chair with tacks. Double piping is used only for decoration, replacing gimp or braid, and should sit next to the show wood where it doesn't protrude.

Piping is made from strips of fabric machine-sewn around a cord, using a piping or zipper foot. You will need to measure the chair for all of the piping that is required and then cut enough strips to stitch together to make up this length. Cut the strips of fabric to 5 cm (2 in) wide on the cross grain (at 45 degrees) if the piping is to go around corners. Otherwise cut the fabric on the straight grain. Keep the type of fabric in mind when cutting on the cross or straight grain – for example, striped fabric always looks better when cut on the cross grain.

Single piping

1 Line up the ruler on the fabric so that 5 cm (2 in) strips can be rotary cut at 45 degrees. Alternatively, mark the fabric with a ruler and pencil and cut along the line with scissors. Cut the ends of the pieces at identical angles so that they can be joined together.

2 Place the first strip of fabric face down on the second strip of fabric and pin them together so that the edges overlap.

3 Machine stitch all the strips together to make a piece long enough for the required length.

4 Place the piping cord on the wrong side of the fabric strip.

5 Fold the fabric strip over the piping cord, hold in place with a horizontal pin, and machine stitch very close to the cord, using a zip foot.

BULKY SEAMS

With thicker fabric, make "V" cuts in the seam allowance to reduce the amount of fabric in the join. Then press the seams open with your fingers (left).

Carefully machine stitch over the join (right).

Double piping

For double piping, use an industrial machine and a double-piping foot. Cut the strips of fabric 13 mm (½ in) wider than for single piping to allow for the extra cord.

1 Stitch a row of piping the same as for single piping using a zip foot. Trim the piece of fabric close to the stitched line.

2 Take a second piece of piping cord, place it beside the original row, and bring the fabric over the top.

3 Keeping the fabric taut over the cord, sew down the middle between the two rows. Use a double-piping foot.

Tools and materials

- **Sewing machine**

- **Fabric**

- **Zip:** measure back plus 15 cm (6 in)

- **Tape measure**

- **Scissors**

- **Pins**

- **Piping:** made to match or contrast

- **Pencil**

Measuring tape

✳ UPHOLSTERER'S TIP
Make a mark or snip in the centre of each side of the top and bottom fabric pieces to help match them up later.

Scissors

Making box cushions

Armchairs and settees sometimes have box cushions on the seat and the back to make them higher and more comfortable. These cushions have a lining filled with foam, feathers, polyester, or a mixture.

Your box cushion should fit neatly onto the seat of the chair with a piped edge on the top and bottom to stop the seams from wearing. Make the foam at least 10 cm (4 in) deep for maximum comfort. Insert a zip at the back of the cushion so the cover can be removed and washed. The zip should go around the back corners and down the sides several centimetres to prevent the cushion from tearing when it is inserted. A pocket for the zip will keep it out of sight. Take care when cutting the fabric for the top and bottom walls to ensure the pattern matches up evenly – especially when using striped fabric.

Measuring the cushion fabric

Two pieces of fabric should be cut for the cushion top and bottom. Allow an extra 13 mm (½ in) seam allowance all round. Cut two pieces of fabric for the cushion wall, allowing the same seam allowance plus an extra 2.5 cm (1 in) width in the section where the zip is to be inserted. The length of the two wall pieces when joined should be 15–20 cm (6–8 in) longer than the circumference of the cushion. The zip should always be positioned at the back of the cushion.

Above: finished cushion with contrasting piping

Making the cover

Sew the piping to the top and bottom components of the cushion, lining up the raw edges. Then, sew the cushion wall first to the top and then to the bottom, ensuring that the corners line up with each other.

1 Take the top or bottom piece of fabric. Start at the middle of the back of the fabric and line up the raw edges of the fabric and the piping. Begin stitching about 7.5 cm (3 in) from the end and machine stitch close to the line of stitching on the piping.

Secure the fabric with the needle in the down position and pull the piping round to realign the raw edges (as seen left).

2 Stop sewing about 7.5 cm (3 in) from the corner, and leave the machine needle in the down position. Make a diagonal cut in the piping from the corner of the main fabric to the stitched line of the piping.

3 Sew to this cut point, leaving the needle in the down position.

4 Turn the fabric and piping 90 degrees so that raw edges are lined up again. Continue stitching around the corner and then down the straight side of the cushion.

5 Repeat these four steps with the other three corners and stop stitching at least 15 cm (6 in) from where you started. Cut the piping so that the two ends overlap by several centimetres.

Joining the piping

Join the piping with a discreet diagonal seam.

1 Undo the machine stitching several centimetres at both ends of the cord.

2 Cut the ends of the fabric diagonally so that they overlap. Make sure that both diagonals go in the same direction and join them together with a pin.

3 Machine sew the join.

Cut a "V" shape out of either side of the seam to remove excess fabric and help the seam lie flat (as seen, right).

4 Lay the cord over the fabric join and cut between the two.

5 Fold the fabric over the cord, lay it flat on the cushion piece, and machine sew together. Take the other piece of fabric and repeat the steps to make the cover and join the piping.

Attaching a zip end

Cushions come in varying sizes so it is best to buy zips by the metre or yard, which can then be cut to size. A zip end is required for each cut length.

1 Make diagonal cuts at the end of the zip, leaving one end longer than the other.

2 Attach zip end first on the long side and then on the shorter side.

3 Holding both ends in one hand gently pull zip end down zip.

Inserting the zip

The wider piece of cushion (as seen, above) has been cut in two lengthwise to accommodate the zipper.

To make the cushion reversible, insert the zip into the cushion wall rather than the cushion bottom. Insert the zip along the back wall and extend it at least 7.5 cm (3 in) around either side. The zip ends come separately and are attached as shown on page 110.

1 Having cut the strip of fabric in two, attach the zipper to one side. Fold the fabric over, pin and tack the zip in place before machine stitching.

2 Now machine stitch the second piece of fabric to the zip stitching in the same direction as strip 1. Hold the ends of the zip together while stitching to ensure that they align correctly. Then join the two pieces of cushion wall together at both ends to make a circle, and attach to the cushion top.

Joining the wall to the top of the cushion

1 With the cushion wall on top, line up the raw edges of cushion top and wall, positioning the zip part at the back of the cushion. Machine stitch these together starting several centimetres from the zip end. Fold the excess fabric of the cushion wall into a pleat.

2 Machine stitch over this fold.

3 Repeat steps 1 and 2 on the cushion wall and bottom, making sure that the centre marks and corners are lined up on the top and the bottom. Machine stitch with the wall on the top as before.

Tools and materials

- **Gimp or braid**
- **Gimp pins**
- **Decorative cord**
- **Slipping thread:** on which to sew cord.
- **Glue gun or fabric glue:** to attach the trimming.
- **Coloured gimp pins:** to anchor the trimming at start and finish. Colour to match top fabric.
- **Scissors**

❋ UPHOLSTERER'S TIP
If the gimp has hot glue on it, take care when pressing it down. You don't want to burn yourself.

Finishing the chair

Braid and gimp are used to cover raw edges of top fabric when it has been trimmed near to the show wood. The braid or gimp should complement the top fabric in colour and texture. A decorative cord is used as a decorative trim or to disguise a join in the top fabric.

Gimp or braid is found on chairs with their show wood exposed. It can be glued or tacked into place using gimp pins, and occasionally it is sewn on by hand. Use decorative or trimming cord instead of piping on scroll edges to disguise a seam in the fabric. The most common type of trimming is a scroll gimp, which has a loop to go around

curves and corners, unlike a straight braid. Before attaching the gimp, you will need to check that the trimming is wide enough to cover the tacks anchoring the top fabric and make adjustments accordingly. A trimming can also be made from a narrow tube of matching fabric anchored to the chair with decorative nails.

Attaching braid or gimp

Measure the chair for the length of trimming needed, and add a further 2.5 cm (1 in) at either end for turnings. Heat the glue gun if using one. Where the trimming needs to be joined, butt the joints together in the centre of the rail rather than joining at the corner.

1 Starting at the back corner, put a little glue on the right side of the trimming about 2.5 cm (1 in) from the end.

2 Place this end face down on the chair, covering the raw edge of the fabric and the tacks or staples. Press down.

3 Insert a coloured gimp pin in the end of the trimming and fold it back so that the right side is now on top.

4 Spread glue along 7.5–10 cm (3–4 in) of trimming and press down. Repeat all along trimming to within 10 cm (4 in) of the end.

5 To finish off, cut the trimming 2.5 cm (1 in) longer than the required length. Fold it over and glue down. An optional gimp pin can be tacked in to secure this end.

USING GIMP PINS

MITRED CORNER

When the trimming has to go around a corner, it needs to be mitred. Insert a gimp pin in the corner and then fold braid or gimp over. Glue down.

Gimp pins are available in several colours: use to finish a braid, or to anchor it firmly to a mitred corner.

Attaching underside barrier cloth

To finish the chair, you should attach a barrier cloth to its underside. This will neaten up all edges and act as an effective dust barrier. Chairs that have tacks inserted on the underside should be finished off with a close weave fabric, such as platform lining or a synthetic platform cloth. Hessian is sometimes used but it does not make an effective dust barrier because of its open weave. Chairs that have polished wood underneath should be left as they are.

Follow these steps to attach the barrier cloth:

1. Turn the chair upside down and use padded trestles or a table to support the arms. Secure all the tacks.
2. Trim any excess fabric.
3. Cut a piece of black lining fabric large enough to cover the base of the chair, allowing an extra 2.5 cm (1 in) all round for turnings.

4. Turn under the raw edges of the fabric and tack down, using 10 mm (⅜ in) tacks at 5 cm (2 in) intervals. Once again, start tacking in the centre of the back and front of the rails, ensuring that the grain of the fabric is straight from back to front and from side to side.
5. At the corners of the legs, fold the fabric back, make a diagonal cut to the corner, and trim away any excess.

Tools and materials

- Domed or decorative nails

- Nail strip and matching nails

- Tacks or gimp pins

- Hammer, preferably rubber-tipped

- Chalk

Hammer

Close nailing and adding a nail strip

Close nailing and nail strips cover the cut edges of leather or vinyl chairs. They come in a brass or antique-bronze finish and are used instead of a gimp or braid. Decorative nails can be bought in many colours and shapes and are used on the front of a leg – to anchor the fabric, for example.

Close nailing is time-consuming and an exacting task for the amateur upholsterer. The nails need to touch each other in an exact line. Only one has to be out of place to ruin the effect. Care also has to be taken with the wood as the tack's holes can damage the edge of the frame. Creating a gauge can make the task easier. A nail strip is a strip of faux nail heads butted up to each other with holes at intervals along the strip for a matching nail to be inserted. The strips come in metre lengths (or yard lengths) with different sized holes and different finishes, so make sure you use matching nails.

Side view of metal gadget

Nails fit into a slot in the gadget.

Front view of gadget

When closing nailing, amateurs are advised to nail to a chalk line, and to make holes with a bradawl to mark the spot for each nail. The nails should be evenly spaced or touching. Gimp pins can be used instead of tacks to tack down the top fabric, as they have a small head. It is important for the domed heads of the nails to cover the line of tacks or staples. Metal hammers can damage the heads of the nails so use either a rubber hammer or cover the head of a metal hammer with a cloth. A gauge can be made (see diagram) and plastic guides are available to buy, but they are not very helpful.

A gadget made from metal is a useful guide for accurate close nailing. These have to be made specially, as only plastic ones are available to purchase. The cantilevered handle lets you get a grip, while the nail is hammered home.

Attaching a nail strip

Nail strip is available in metre (yard) length strips in either a bronze or a brass finish, with matching domed nails. Each strip has 10 holes for the domed nails.

1 Holding the strip in one hand, place a domed nail in the first hole and hammer it home. Take special care if you're using a metal hammer instead of a rubber-tipped one.

2 Repeat this on subsequent holes.

3 Where the strips need joining then overlap two holes.

Nails with a decorative domed head (as seen, left) can be used individually to anchor fabric instead of tacks and gimp or braid.

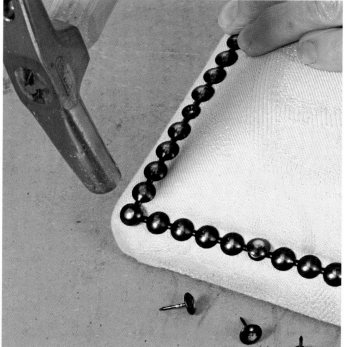

4 Hammer a nail through the two holes to complete the join.

Types of furniture

A variety of different chairs and sofas – from traditional to modern – are featured in this section together with a description of their upholstery, a list of the materials used, a cutting plan and a comprehensive calculation of the amount of fabric you will require for each piece. Instruction on how to measure the different components is also included.

How to use cutting plans

First, use a soft tape measure to calculate the components needed to re-cover the chair. Record these on a chart. The measurements given on the following pages are only estimates and should, therefore, be used simply as a guide. When all the measurements have been recorded, transfer them to a cutting plan. The total figure at the bottom of the left-hand column is the amount of fabric required.

For more information on how to use cutting plans see page 92. The abbreviations used in this section are explained on page 9.

Dining chairs
Edwardian chair with a drop-in seat

DINING CHAIR VARIATIONS

Wooden seat frame with solid plywood base This is the ideal beginner's project. Decide what density foam you'd like, then use a spray adhesive to put a layer of polyester on top. Finally, stretch the cover over and attach with staples or tacks.

Seat with zigzag springs Following the plans laid out in this book, put on the layers of padding, then calico, and the final fabric covering. You don't have to stick to traditional fabrics – use whatever strikes your fancy.

Drop-in seat with coil springs This is a lot like the seat with zigzag springs, but purists would tend to keep the fabric on this one traditional.

The Edwardian dining chair, introduced in the early 1900s, was usually made from beech or oak and stained to look like mahogany, walnut or rosewood. The chairs were often reproductions of the Victorian period, mass produced and upholstered traditionally.

Weave is straight from front to back and side to side.

Stuffing on sides should be smooth and not have any lumps.

Neatly pleated corners.

Seat stuffing is domed in the centre.

Fabric is stretched over the seat.

Anatomy

The drop-in seat is an ideal project for the beginner. The seat can be removed from the chair – where it fits neatly into the chair rails – so it is an easily transportable project. Upholstering the drop-in seat teaches the beginner the rudiments of upholstery, webbing, attaching hessian and basic hair stuffing. The webbing is attached to the top of the frame to form a base for the hessian. Bridles are stitched onto the hessian to hold the stuffing of hair, coir or black fibre, and then covered with a layer of white cotton wadding and calico. The calico is stretched tightly over the hair and tacked on the underside of the frame. Then the black platform fabric is tacked to the underneath of the frame to cover the raw edges and tacks. Occasionally chairs have short coil springs in the base. Modern chairs can have zigzag springs, or on very basic chairs, a base of plywood. In these cases, use foam or rubberized hair to upholster.

❏ SEE ALSO
Webbing, page 40; Preparing a hessian base, page 58; First stuffings, page 68.

Thumbnail guide for taking measurements

components	Length		Width		number required
	cm	in	cm	in	
seat	56	22	61	24	1

KEY

— = *Width*

— = *Length*

✳ UPHOLSTERER'S TIP
When attaching calico to drop-in seats, keep the sides free of any stuffing so that the frame will fit into the chair when finished.

Fabric required

Plain or patterned fabric for 1 or 2 chairs: 0.6 m (2 ft)
Plain or patterned fabric for 3 or 4 chairs: 1.2 m (3.9 ft)

Extra material may be required for the 3 or 4 chairs to be identical. Upholstery fabric is normally 137 cm (54 in) wide.

Measure the seat from underneath the rail at the back and front, and from side to side. A remnant of fabric is ideal for one chair as it is sometimes only possible to buy fabric by the metre. Buying fabric becomes more economical when covering multiple seats – the width of the purchased fabric will generally be enough for two seats, and approximately 1.2 m (3.9 ft) will cover four seats.

If the fabric has a large pattern, place it in the centre of the chair and cut two identical pieces from the width. When there are four or more seats, consider the placement of the pattern on the chair.

1 Seat

Total: 0.6 m/ 2 ft

4 Seats

Total: 1.2 m/ 3.9 ft

Centralize these pieces if using a large-patterned fabric.

Stuffed over-seats
Balloon-back stuffed over-seats

STUFFED OVER-SEAT VARIATIONS

Stuffed over-seat piano stool This design would suit a cream trellis-weave textile.

Prayer stool (note the sloping angle of the stool for kneeling on). Usually covered in leather, for long-lasting wear. Seen in smaller, much older churches in needlepoint, sometimes displaying parishioners' names.

Round piano stool This piece turns in both directions to go higher or lower and usually comes with claw feet. Also could be used as a dressing table stool.

A Victorian balloon-back dining chair has a stuffed over-seat and is upholstered using traditional materials and methods.

Fabric stretched over chair

Corners without a pleat

Gimp covering raw edges of fabric

Small pattern centred

Fabric tucked into corner

Anatomy

An upholstered stuffed over-seat, like the Victorian balloon-back dining chair, has many of the basic principles of traditional upholstery and is a good project for the beginner. It is easily transportable and will provide the beginner with the skills to advance to bigger projects. The seat has a webbed base covered with hessian, rather than springs. The first stuffing and stitched edge are of hair or fibre, and the second stuffing is normally of hair. These stuffings are covered with white cotton wadding and calico before the top fabric is added. The top fabric is stapled down to the show wood frame, and two tulip style pleats finish the rounded corners. The fabric is trimmed close to the show wood, and the raw edges are covered with a gimp or braid attached with a hot-glue gun. The chair's underside should only be covered with a barrier cloth if there are tack marks to be concealed.

❏ SEE ALSO
Webbing, page 40; First stuffings, page 68; Stitching an edge, page 80; Second stuffings, page 86; Attaching new coverings, page 94; Finishing the chair, page 112.

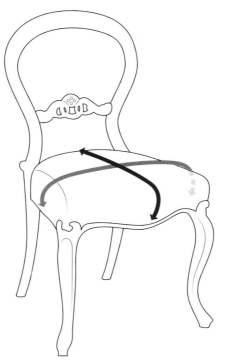

Thumbnail guide for taking measurements

components	Length		Width		number required
	cm	in	cm	in	
SEAT	66	26	68	27	1

※ UPHOLSTERER'S TIP
If you are only covering one chair, check to see if a fabric shop has a remnant for sale – this will be enough to do the job and cheaper than buying a whole metre.

KEY
━━━ = Width
━━━ = *Length*

Fabric required

Plain fabric for 1 or 2 chairs:
0.7 m (2.3 ft)
Plain fabric for 3 or 4 chairs:
1.5 m (4.5 ft)
Patterned fabric for 1 or 2 chairs:
1 m (3 ft)
Patterned fabric for 3 or 4 chairs:
2 m (6.6 ft)

The measurements of an average-size stuffed overseat are: length 66 cm (26 in) and width 68 cm (27 in). Fabric is (usually) 137 cm (54 in) wide, so two seats can be cut from one width of fabric. If the seat requires more than 68 cm (27 in), then only one can be cut from the width. The cutting plans indicate the fabric required for up to four chairs with both plain and patterned fabric. It is more economical to buy fabric for a multiple of chairs rather than single ones. Choose patterned fabric with a centred pattern. If the chair has show wood at the front and sides, use a matching gimp to cover the raw edge of fabric.

1 Chair

Plain fabric total: 0.7 m/ 2.3 ft
Large patterned fabric Total: 0.9 m/ 3 ft

2 Chairs

137/ 54

68/ 27   68/ 27

66/ 26   1   1   90/ 36

Plain fabric total: 0.7 m/ 2.5 ft
Large patterned fabric total: 0.9 m/ 3 ft

4 Chairs

Plain fabric total: 1.5 m/ 4.5 ft
Large patterned fabric Total: 2 m/ 6.6 ft

Armchairs
Small Victorian armchair

Small winged chair This great little chair works in areas that are challenging due to lack of space. You can upholster it to fit in with the existing room style.

Wooden seat frame with solid plywood base This has a mahogany frame covered in leather. This is a chair that will be re-covered many times in its life.

Early Victorian armchair This elegant seat has a cord above the lumber part of the back and fringing at the front.

This small and traditionally upholstered armchair has tapered front legs and deep buttoned arms.

Stitched roll on the top joining up with the arms

Deep buttons on arms

Covered buttons

Piping at the bottom edge

Contrasting fabric piped edge

Anatomy

This Victorian armchair has a fully upholstered seat, back and arms. The seat is sprung with nine coil springs on a webbed base. It has two stuffings of hair and a deep, firm, stitched edge at the front. The back has no springs, but two stuffings of hair and a stitched roll on the top edge. White cotton wadding and calico cover the stuffings of hair on the seat and the back, the calico being tightly stretched and tacked down. Since the chair is narrow, the arms have only a thin stuffing of hair and a covering of white cotton wadding and calico. The top of the arms has a stitched edge and the top cover has three deep buttons that take the fabric around the arm's curve. The roll on the arms joins up with the roll on the top of the back.

❏ SEE ALSO
Webbing, page 40; Springing, page 46;
Preparing a hessian base, page 58; First
stuffings, page 68; Stitching an edge, page
80; Second stuffings, page 86; Attaching
new coverings, page 94; Deep buttoning, 98;
Making single and double piping, 106.

**Thumbnail guide for
taking measurements**

KEY
= *Width*
= *Length*

| components | Length | | Width | | number |
	cm	in	cm	in	required
SEAT	81	32	81	32	1
I. BACK	76	30	63	25	1
O. BACK	61	24	63	25	1
I. ARM	66	26	74	29	2
O.ARM	61	24	68	27	2
TOP OF ARM	30	12	99	39	2

Fabric required

Plain fabric: 3.5 m (11.5 ft)
Patterned fabric: 4.1 m (13.5 ft)

Use a plain or small patterned fabric
for this chair, since a large pattern
would be lost on the small inside
arms and in the deep buttoning
on the arms. The pictured chair has
piping made from a check fabric
that has been cut on the bias. It's
tacked to the frame, and the top
fabric is slip stitched to it. The
piping along the bottom of the
chair is tacked on the underneath
of the frame and dustcover fabric
covers the raw edges. Allow extra
fabric for the sloping angle on the
width of the arms. The fabric on the
top of the arm can be taken from
the length or width, depending
on the pattern. Allow 0.5 m (20 in)
extra fabric for the piping when
using patterned fabric.

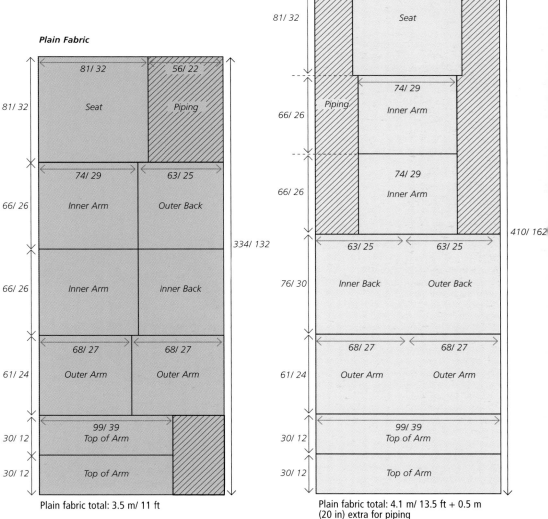

Plain Fabric

Plain fabric total: 3.5 m/ 11 ft

Patterned Fabric

Plain fabric total: 4.1 m/ 13.5 ft + 0.5 m
(20 in) extra for piping

Armchairs
Victorian spoon-back chair

ARMCHAIR VARIATIONS

Ladies chair with cabriole legs This deep-buttoned, armless chair enabled a lady to sit to arrange her petticoats. This 19th-century piece is an elegant classic.

Spoon-back chair with plain back Also known as an "elbow chair", this can be used at the dining table.

Spoon-back chair with deep-buttoned back This mid-19th century piece usually comes with lovely carved details on arms, legs and top of back.

This oak-framed Victorian armchair has a sprung seat and deep-buttoned arms and back.

Buttons on back in diamond pattern

Third button on arm hides join in fabric

Carving of oak leaf on top of arm

Braid attached just above show wood

Carved and stout legs indicate a chair's high quality

Angle of back legs indicates superior quality

Anatomy

Coil springs are stitched to the webbing base and covered with hessian and two stuffings of hair. There is a stitched edge at the front and a covering of white cotton wadding and calico prior to the top cover. The deep-buttoned back is formed with a thick layer of hair on a hessian base with a stitched edge all around; this gives the back a definite shape. White cotton wadding and polyester wadding cover the back, and a stitched edge around the carved show wood details the arms. The outside back and arms are covered with hessian and the top cover. A glued-on gimp or braid covers the raw edges on the front and back.

❏ SEE ALSO
Webbing, page 40; Springing, page 46; Working a sprung edge, page 54; Preparing a hessian base, page 58; First stuffings, page 68; Stitching an edge, page 80; Second stuffings, page 86; Attaching new coverings, page 94; Deep buttoning, 98; Finishing the chair, page 112.

Thumbnail guide for taking measurements

KEY

———	= Width
━━━	= Length

components	Length		Width		number required
	cm	in	cm	in	
SEAT	81	32	81	32	1
I. BACK	102	40	81	32	1
O. BACK	86	34	76	30	1
I. ARM	66	26	61	24	2
O. ARM	41	16	51	20	2

Fabric required

3.2 m (10.5 ft) plain fabric
3.9 m (12.8 ft) patterned fabric

Work out the fabric by imagining the chair flat. The pile of the fabric should go from top to bottom, on the seat from back to front, and on the arms from the top of the arm down to the seat. Allow extra fabric for the buttoned area – 4 cm (1.5 in) per button. Use seven pattern pieces to cover the chair. Fold the arm fabric over the back fabric at the back of the arm, and secure it with a button. Slip stitch the outside arm to the outside back down the line of the back rails. Because of the deep buttoning and the size of the seat, you will need extra material for a large patterned fabric. Stripes and large patterns become distorted with the buttoning, so an all-over random pattern is recommended.

The components for the arms on the cutting plan for patterned fabric are cut larger in width to allow the pattern to be centralized.

Plain Fabric

137/ 54

82/ 32 — Seat
55/ 22 — Outer Arm   42/ 16
Outer Arm   42/ 16
82/ 32

102/ 40 — Inner Back

316/ 124

76/ 30 — Outer Back
61/ 24
86/ 34
1.4m Inner Arm   66/ 26

1.4m Inner Arm   66/ 26
46/ 18

Plain fabric total: 3.2 m/ 10.5 ft

Patterned Fabric

137/ 54

28/ 11   82/ 32   28/ 11
82/ 32
Seat

102/ 40 — Inner Back

378/ 148

55/ 22   55/ 22
66/ 26 — Inner Arm   Inner Arm

42/ 16 — Outer Arm   Outer Arm

43/ 17   76/ 30   43/ 17
86/ 34   Outer Back

Patterned fabric total: 3.9 m/ 12.8 ft

Armchairs
Victorian horseshoe chair

ARMCHAIR VARIATIONS

Horseshoe chair with curved back
Castors allow the chair to roll smoothly. Look for a cream velour or green leather, to show off the rosewood legs.

Horseshoe chair with curved buttoned back and seat A buttoner's dream, this piece is ordinarily covered in leather. It's perfect for a pub, club, library, family room or den.

Horseshoe chair with upholstered back and arms Another one for a leather cover, although don't restrict yourself to black. Make sure the show wood is clean and polished, and the nails properly spaced and aligned.

The Victorian horseshoe chair, or library chair, has a sprung seat, a curved, deep-buttoned back and upholstered arms.

Decorative cord covers stitching

Buttons symmetrically positioned

Arm and back slip stitched together

Gimp hides tacked edge

Fully sprung seat with stitches at front

Neatly pleated corners.

Gimp around front

Anatomy

The horseshoe chair comes in several slightly different styles. The style shown above has a coil sprung seat and a stuffing of hair, white cotton wadding and calico with a stitched edge along the front edge. The back has a stitched edge around the two scroll ends and along the top of the back, which gives it its shape. It has seven deep buttons. The stitched edge on the arms stabilizes the stuffing and gives the arms shape. When upholstering, take care to make the arms of the chair identical. Instead of piping, decorative cord is stitched on the back's scroll ends. The raw edges of fabric at the front and arms are covered with gimp, which is glued on using a hot-glue gun.

❑ See also
Webbing, page 40; Springing, page 46; First stuffings, page 68; Stitching an edge, page 80; Second stuffings, page 86; Attaching new coverings, page 94; Finishing the chair, page 112.

Thumbnail guide for taking measurements

	Length		Width		
components	**cm**	**in**	**cm**	**in**	**number required**
SEAT	92	36	96	38	1
I. BACK	72	28	71	28	1
O. BACK	26	10	50	20	1
ARMS	26	10	46	18	2
FACINGS	20	8	15	6	2

KEY

——— = Width
——— = Length

❋ Upholsterer's Tip
When you upholster the arms, use two pieces of calico the same size to make the arms identical.

❋ Upholsterer's Tip
Use extra material if you plan to make piping instead of using a decorative cord.

Fabric required

1.7 m (5.6 ft) plain or patterned fabric

Large patterned fabric is not ideal for the Victorian horseshoe chair because of the deep buttoning and narrow arms. Instead, use fabric with a self or small asymmetrical pattern. The chair has seven fabric components: the seat, inside back, outside back, arms and two facings. To figure out which way the fabric should go on the arms, imagine the chair is flat. You will see that the length of the fabric goes from top to bottom and the width from side to side – as the diagram shows. The fabric on the arm is slip stitched to the back fabric. The fabric on the scroll end is stuffed with wadding and slip stitched into place.

Plain Fabric

Patterned Fabric

Plain fabric total: 1.7 m/ 5.6 ft

Patterned fabric total: 1.7 m/ 5.6 ft + extra 0.5 m (20 in) if piping required.

Bedroom armchairs
Modern bedroom chair

BEDROOM CHAIR VARIATIONS

Modern bedroom chair with upholstered seat and back
Contemporary in style, but works as an all-purpose chair. Uses clean lines with no frills. Perfect as additional seating.

Bedroom chair with curved seat and shaped back From the Art-Deco period, this piece has an overstuffed seat and three-channelled back. At home at a dressing table.

Slipper chair This piece has no arms and works with or without a loose seat cushion. It nicely shows off the woodwork of the legs and also gives a sense of space, as you "look through" the chair.

This chair is upholstered with foam or rubberized hair and has a box-pleated skirt. It's covered with a check fabric.

Back tacking strip

Seat fabric stretched tightly

Box pleats

Anatomy

Modern materials make up the upholstery on this basic chair. However, rubber webbing and foam do not have a long life span; replace them after a few years. Rubber webbing is used as the base and is stapled to the top of the frame. In better quality chairs the rubber webbing has metal fixing-clips attached to the ends, which fit into slots on the top of the seat frame. Fire-retardant foam and a protective layer of polyester wadding cover the foam. Calico is stretched over the webbing, which helps to take the pressure off the top fabric. The top fabric is tacked or stapled to the outside edge of the seat frame. The skirt is either gathered or pleated and is made up prior to attaching. It is then back tacked onto the side rail of the chair.

❑ SEE ALSO
*Webbing, page 40; Springing, page 46;
Stitching an edge, page 80; Preparing a hessian
base, 58; Second stuffings, page 86; Attaching
new coverings, page 94.*

components	Length cm	in	Width cm	in	number required
SEAT	66	26	66	26	1
I. BACK	71	28	68	27	1
O. BACK	61	24	56	22	1
VALANCE PLEATED	36	14	274	108	1

Thumbnail guide for taking measurements

KEY

	= Width
	= Length

Fabric required

2 m (6.6 ft) plain or patterned fabric

If using check fabric on this chair, cut the piping on the
cross grain. Attach the seat and back with staples or
tacks, and tack the outside back on the top. Slip stitch
down the sides. Line the skirt with curtain lining or
calico, which you need to make up before attaching.
This includes the piping, which is machine-stitched to the
top edge of the skirt. Measure the circumference of the
chair and make the skirt to fit. The cutting plan allows for
double the measurement of the circumference of the chair
for the valance.

Plain and Patterned

Total: 2 m/ 6.6 ft

Winged armchairs
Modern winged fireside chair

WINGED CHAIR VARIATIONS

Modern rocker chair with loose seat cushion This chair looks good in any covering: dress it up in a classic paisley; toughen it up in leather; playful in plaid.

Modern upholstered wing chair with skirt The perfect place for grandma to read to her small grandchild.

Modern wing chair with curved wings and curved front facings This piece has a buttoned back to sink into, and will always look good covered in a duck egg soft blue-green.

Modern upholstery methods are used for this winged fireside chair.

The upholsterer thought it would be fun to re-upholster this winged chair in a patchwork of coordinating textiles. The cutting plan (opposite) assumes that you will be working with a single length of fabric.

Piping on the wings cut on the cross weave.

Edge or tack roll around outline of arms and wings

Piped edge at top and bottom of cushion

Loose box cushion made of foam

Edge or tack roll around seat front.

Piped edge to front facings

Anatomy

This winged armchair dating from around 1940 has been upholstered using rubberized hair rather than real hair, coir or fibre. This is covered by a layer of wool and cotton wadding, calico, and then the top fabric. Coil springs have been used on the seat and back. Staples have been used throughout instead of tacks. There are no stitched edges but an edge, or tack roll, has been used to form a foundation along the front edge of the seat, and around the edge of the arms and wings. The cushion is made of foam and the cushion cover has a zip that is positioned at the back of the cushion and extends round both back corners for ease of inserting the cushion pad.

❏ SEE ALSO

Springing, page 46; Preparing a hessian base, page 58; First stuffings, page 68; Stitching an edge, page 80; Second stuffings, page 86; Attaching new coverings, page 94; Making box cushions, page 108.

Thumbnail guide for taking measurements

KEY

━━━ = Width
━━━ = Length

components	Length		Width		number required
	cm	in	cm	in	
I. BACK	91	36	68	27	1
O. BACK	76	30	68	27	1
I. ARM	56	22	69	27	2
O.ARM	36	14	61	24	2
I. WING	51	20	36	14	2
O. WING	46	18	31	12	2
CUSHION	61	24	56	22	2
CUSHION WALL 1	13	5	137	54	1
2	13	6	137	54	1
FRONT FACING	31	12	91	36	1
ARM FACING	46	18	20	8	2

Fabric required

3.5 m (11.5 ft) plain fabric
4.1 m (13.5 ft) patterned fabric

A hard-wearing fabric with a high rub test would be most suitable for this chair if it is to be well used. There are 17 fabric components, and if the fabric has a large pattern plan, cut it out carefully. An extra metre will ensure the pattern repeat can be centred. Make sure the weave of the fabric is vertical when applying all components (especially the inside and outside wings). The fabric on the back of the wing needs to line up with the outside arm. The T-shaped cushion has a piped edge top and bottom and a zip at the back. Make a spring cover to cover the tension springs.

Plain Fabric

Patterned Fabric

Plain fabric total: 3.7 m/ 12 ft

Patterned fabric total: 4.1 m/ 13.5 ft

Nursing chairs
Victorian nursing chair

NURSING CHAIR VARIATIONS

Deep-buttoned nursing chair
A beautiful, classic piece of furniture. You don't need to be a nursing mother to appreciate the plush upholstery and comfortable fit.

Victorian nursing chair upholstered over bottom rail With its top to bottom channels, this one will test your upholstery skills, but it will be your reward to enjoy it.

Late Victorian nursing chair with fabric joined at the centre and side facings A lovely rolled back with sturdy base and legs makes this perfect in the bedroom – graceful and comfy.

This small nursing chair has a curved seat. The fabric on the back is in three pieces and is joined underneath the cord.

Fabric joined here

Scroll edges at top and bottom

Cord glued to hide tacks

Outside back stitched to piping

Brass finials covering screws

Decorative cord used instead of piping

Anatomy

The seat and the back of this chair are made from one piece of fabric. The curve of the chair makes it difficult to tighten the top fabric without any creases. The chair can be buttoned with either deep or shallow buttoning, or two vertical rows of stitching; the stitching hidden with a decorative cord. The stuffing on the sides of the chair is stitched into a small roll using a large curved needle instead of a long double pointed one. The seat is upholstered without springs. The outside-back piping is stapled on both sides. The fabric at the top is carded and slip stitched to the piping, and then tacked onto the bottom rail. The underneath of the chair can be covered with a coloured platform lining or a scrap of available fabric.

❏ See also
*Webbing, page 40; Preparing a hessian base,
page 58; First stuffings, page 68; Stitching an
edge, page 80; Second stuffings, page 86;
Attaching new coverings, page 94; Making
single and double piping, page 106; Finishing
the chair, page 112.*

**Thumbnail guide for taking
measurements**

components	Length		Width		number required
	cm	**in**	**cm**	**in**	
FRONT	117	46	51	20	1
O. BACK	56	22	38	15	1

KEY

————— = Width
————— = Length

Fabric required

1.2 m (4 ft) plain or patterned fabric

The same amount of fabric is required whether it is plain or patterned, but
because the chair is narrow, a plain or small pattern is advisable. Use only two
pieces of fabric for this chair, which can be cut from the width of the fabric.
The length used for the seat determines the amount of fabric you will need,
and offcut pieces of piping can be used. Stitch two vertical rows and tighten
the fabric down the centre so there are no creases. Tack or staple the side
pieces onto the frame next to the show wood. Use extra fabric if the chair is
to be deep buttoned, allowing 13 mm (½ in) extra between each button on
width and length. Glue decorative cord onto the raw edges of fabric.

❋ Upholsterer's Tip
*If using a patterned fabric on
this chair, it is advisable to use
a small, random pattern so that
the joins are not obvious.*

Plain Fabric

Plain fabric total: 1.2 m/ 4 ft

Patterned Fabric

Patterned fabric total: 1.2 m/ 4 ft

Wood frames
Pin-cushion seats and backs

Stool or window seat This seat from the mid-18th century, requires a very thin padded cushion. It is a piece that can fit anywhere: at your dressing table, piano or at the foot of the bed.

Chair back This Art-Nouveau piece would suit contemporary fabric selections. The chair would serve you well in the hall or conservatory.

Folding chair Add a pin-cushion chair pad and take the chair outside – to the beach, the park, wherever. Casual is the attitude.

A pin-cushion seat has a very thin layer of padding on the top of the frame and is finished off with gimp or braid.

Corners without a pleat

Fabric smooth at sides

Braid attached to hide raw edges

Anatomy

A wood-frame chair with a pin-cushion seat is another ideal project for the beginner. The base of the seat can be a piece of plywood or a frame that needs webbing. Before you upholster, note where the black platform lining was attached. If there are no tack marks underneath the chair, then the black fabric would have been on the top of the frame, so attach this first. If there are marks underneath, then the black fabric is added last. If the black fabric is to go on the top, anchor it first with a few tacks followed by webbing, hessian, a thin layer of hair, white cotton wadding and calico. When you tighten the calico, make sure the edges have a smooth slope so there is no necessity for a pleat at the corners.

❏ SEE ALSO
Webbing, page 40; First stuffings, page 68; Attaching new coverings, page 94; Finishing the chair, page 112.

components	Length		Width		number required
	cm	in	cm	in	
SEAT	53	21	53	21	1

Thumbnail guide for taking measurements

KEY

━━━ = *Width*
━━━ = *Length*

Fabric required

Plain or patterned fabric for 1 or 2 chairs: 0.6 m (2 ft)
Plain or patterned fabric 3 or 4 chairs 1.1 m (3.6 ft)

Extra material may be required if the pattern match is large and an identical pattern is required on each seat. Measure from the back of the seat to the front, and from one side to the other. If the seat is small, it may be possible to cut the fabric for three seats from one width.

When using patterned fabric, cut extra so the pattern can be centred on the seat. With a corner chair, the fabric will run from the back corner to the front corner; it's best to use a larger piece of fabric because of the raw edges on the cross weave of the fabric, and to accommodate for stretching. To prevent stretching, temporarily tack the corners and then the centre of the sides, gradually working out to the corners. Measure around the four sides of the seat to work out how much braid or gimp is required, adding 5 cm (2 in) for turnings. Then make the join of the braid or gimp at the back corner with the two ends of braid or gimp butted together.

1–2 Chairs

Total: 0.6 m/ 2 ft

4 Chairs

Total: 1.1 m/ 3.6 ft

Components centralized when using patterned fabric.

Wood frames
Modern chair with wooden frame

Modern chair with curved back and arm rail This chair is similar to a modern mid-20th-century boardroom chair. Perfect with green leather.

Modern chair with two cushions and arm pads This is a great chair for the library, which would best suit a tapestry fabric.

Modern chair with round seat and upholstered back pad This contemporary style is best used in commercial settings, such as conference and meeting rooms. Would suit leather or vinyl.

This wooden framed chair might be used in a library or an office. Its back and seat are upholstered with modern materials and methods.

Straight pleat on corner

Fabric going around arm at side

Corner pleat anchored with decorative stud

Anatomy

The seat's zigzag springs are anchored to the chair frame with clips and nails. These are covered with hessian and a piece of 5 cm (2 in) rubberized hair, cut to the shape of the seat. The rubberized hair is secured to the hessian using a spray adhesive. Blue wadding and white cotton wadding are placed on top of the sheet of hair and trimmed away to cover the rough edge of the hair. A tight covering of calico over the wadding is anchored to the underside of the chair with Y-shaped cuts around the arms of the chair, and a diagonal cut into the back corners. The same procedure is used for the back, but with 2.5 cm (1 in) rubberized hair. The top cover is anchored at the back, and the outside back is slip stitched on.

❏ SEE ALSO
*Webbing, page 40; Springing, page 46;
Preparing a hessian base, page 58; First
stuffings, page 68; Attaching new coverings,
page 94; Deep buttoning, 98.*

components	Length		Width		number required
	cm	in	cm	in	
SEAT	66	26	91	36	1
I. BACK	56	22	66	26	1
O. BACK	56	22	50	20	1

Thumbnail guide for taking measurements

KEY

―――― = Width
―――― = Length

Fabric required

**1.3 m (4.3 ft) plain or patterned fabric
0.5 m (20 in) fabric for piping**

The chair is covered with three pieces of fabric – the seat, inside back and outside back.
If the fabric is large-patterned, centralize it on the inside back and the seat. The fabric on
the seat and inside back has a Y-cut around the arms, a diagonal cut at the back corners
and a straight pleat on the front and top corners. Card the outside back at the top and slip
stitch down either side. Plain and large patterned fabric require the same amount of fabric,
but extra may be required if the large pattern is to be centred on the seat and back. Extra
material is required for piping as shown in cutting plan 2 (patterned fabric).

✳ UPHOLSTERER'S TIP
*To create a smooth edge
on top, chamfer the
rubberized hair off the
underneath edge.*

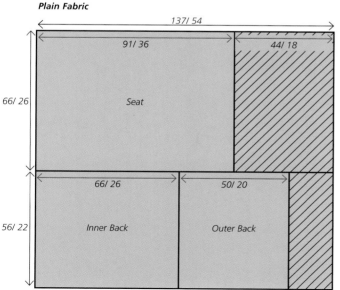

Plain Fabric

Plain fabric total: 1.3 m/ 4 ft

Patterned Fabric

Patterned fabric total: 1.3 m/ 4 ft + 0.5 m (20 in) piping if required

❏ SEE ALSO
Webbing, page 40; Springing, page 46;
Stitching an edge, page 80; Preparing a hessian
base, 58; Second stuffings, page 86; Attaching
new coverings, page 94; Making piping, page
106; Making a box cushion, page 108.

✳ UPHOLSTERER'S TIP
Use a hot-glue gun with
a clear glue stick to glue
braid or gimp to the chair.
The glue is hot and dries
quickly, so have your
equipment on hand before
starting.

Settees
Modern two-seater settee

SETTEE VARIATIONS

19th-century settee This pretty two-seater sofa with sturdy mahogany turned legs would have been upholstered traditionally and finished in a delicate brocade or silk fabric.

Knole settee The Knole settee originated in Kent in the early 18th century. This reproduction piece is made up of square-shaped frames, which are completely upholstered. It has two loose seat cushions and two bolsters. The hinged arms are held in place by decorative tasseled cords.

Modern Knole Settee The deep seat on this piece allows room for large throw pillows (scatter cushions). Use duck feathers in the single seat cushion. Leather is a fabulous covering on this timeless beauty.

This settee has been upholstered with modern methods and has four loose cushions with removable covers.

Back cushions shaped to sit on arm

Front facings machine-stitched with piping to arm piece

Piped edge to cushions

Fitted front facing

Anatomy

The frame of the settee is covered with a thin layer of stuffing so that the cushions are soft and comfortable. The settee is upholstered using zigzag springs on the seat with a covering of hessian and foam or rubberized hair. A layer of wadding and a top cover complete the upholstery. The back and arms follow the same process, but without springs. The deep cushions have three sections filled with qualofil – a polyester fibre filling – which is very hard wearing. The sections prevent the cushion filling from moving inside the case. The zip on the cushions goes along the back wall and several centimetres down either side. Save money by replacing the top fabric underneath the cushions on the seat and back with platform lining. The fabric covering the settee is cotton with a fire-retardant backing.

components	Length cm	Length in	Width cm	Width in	number required
I. BACK	81	32	185	73	1
O. BACK	74	29	167	66	1
FRONT FACING	46	18	137	54	1
I. ARM	76	30	112	44	2
O. ARM	61	24	96	38	2
SEAT CUSHION	69	27	74	29	4
BACK CUSHION	51	20	89	35	4
SEAT WALLS CUSHION	13	5	137	54	2
	13	6	137	54	2
BACK CUSHION WALLS	13	5	137	54	2
	13	6	137	54	2

Fabric required

10.7 m (35 ft) plain or patterned fabric

When using patterned fabric, decide where the pattern will be centralized on each of the components prior to cutting. The extra fabric allowed for piping gives flexibility, so use the cutting pattern as a guide rather than a fixed rule. Pipe the large cushions on the seat and back with the same fabric as on the settee. Pipe the front arm facings, also. All of the piping could be of a contrasting fabric, but make sure it is of a similar thickness as the chair fabric. Join the fabric where the width of the chair or settee is wider than the width of the fabric. Cut the extra length in two and add to either end of the large piece of fabric.

Thumbnail guide for taking measurements

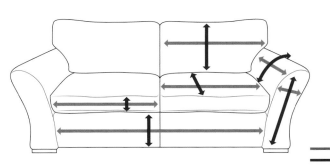

KEY

━━━ = Width
━━━ = Length

Plain Fabric

137/ 54

29	Outer Back
18	Front Facing
3/ 5	
3/ 5	
3/ 5	
3/ 5	Cushion Walls
5/ 6	
5/ 6	
5/ 6	
5/ 6	
32	Inner Back
30	112/ 44 Inner Arm / 25/ 10
30	Inner Arm
24	96/ 38 Outer Arm / 12/ 30 Outer Back Extra / 29/ 74
24	Outer Arm / 29

Sub-total:
587/ 231

137/ 54

51/ 20	89/ 35 Back Cushion	48/ 19 Inner Back / 81/ 32
51/ 20	Back Cushion	
51/ 20	Back Cushion	123/ 48
51/ 20	Back Cushion	
69/ 27	29 Seat Cushion	25 Piping / 137/ 54
69/ 27	Seat Cushion	
69/ 27	Seat Cushion	137/ 54
69/ 27	Seat Cushion	

Sub-total:
480/ 183

Patterned Fabric

137/ 54

46/ 18	Front Facing
50/ 20	
60/ 24	Cushion Walls
81/ 32	Inner Back
76/ 30	112/ 44 Inner Arm
76/ 30	Inner Arm
61/ 24	99/ 38 Outer Arm
61/ 24	Outer Arm

Sub-total:
513/ 202

137/ 54

74/ 29	Outer Back
69/ 27	29 Seat Cushion
69/ 27	Seat Cushion
69/ 27	Seat Cushion
69/ 27	Seat Cushion
51/ 20	35 Back Cushion
51/ 20	Back Cushion
51/ 20	Back Cushion
51/ 20	Back Cushion

Sub-total:
554/ 217

Plain fabric total: 10.7 m/ 35 ft

Patterned fabric total: 10.7 m/ 35 ft

Chaise longues
Traditional deep-buttoned chaise longues

CHAISE LONGUE VARIATIONS

Edwardian chaise with buttoned head This type of chaise is sometimes described as being of inferior quality because of the simplicity of the carving and the somewhat narrow legs. It would have been filled with the cheapest stuffings and covered in a velvet or tapestry.

Regency-style chaise with bolster This type of chaise often only had a base of webbing and hessian covered by top fabric, and a thick squab cushion rather than a fully upholstered and sprung seat. The head has an inward-facing curve and a squab cushion to fit inside.

Day bed These were first introduced in the early 18th century together with chaise longues and were designed for lounging. This example has a deep-buttoned head and seat and would have been upholstered in a comfortable fabric, such as velvet or tapestry.

This comfortable 19th-century chaise longue with tapered legs and castors has deep buttoning on the back and head. There is a sprung edge around the seat, which may have been originally deep-buttoned in a velour, velvet, or damask.

Scroll end

Pattern of buttons following line of arm

Gathered border

Sprung edge all around seat

Decorative cord instead of piping

Anatomy

This chaise longue has a deep-buttoned, fully upholstered head and back, with no show wood. Real hair is used as stuffing under the deep-buttoning, and a stitched edge runs along the top of the head and around the scroll-front facing. Another stitched edge runs along the top of the back to give the back its curved shape. As some of this roll is on a curve, it is best to use loose-weave scrim. The seat uses coil springs and has a sprung edge attached to a wire that runs around the seat to the back arm. This wire and stitched edge form a lip to which the calico and top fabric is stitched. The border is gathered and slip-stitched to the underside of the lip. Decorative cord is then stitched on.

> ✴ UPHOLSTERER'S TIP
> *When deep buttoning, place a layer of polyester wadding over the white cotton wadding to stop cotton breaking up. To prevent a ridge forming around the button, cut a large hole in the polyester where the button is to go.*

❏ SEE ALSO
Stripping, page 34; Webbing, page 40;
Springing, page 46; Working a sprung edge,
page 54; Preparing a hessian base, page 58;
First stuffing, page 68; Stitching an edge, page
80; Second stuffing, page 86; Attaching new
coverings, page 94; Making single and double
piping, page 106; Finishing the chair, page 112.

**Thumbnail guide for taking
measurements**

KEY

	= W. Plan A
	= Alt. L. Plan B
	= L. Plan A
	= Alt. W. Plan B

Fabric required

components	Length		Width		number required
	cm	in	cm	in	
SEAT	97	38	180	71	1
ALTERNATIVE SEAT	180	71	97	38	1
I. ARM	102	40	268	106	1
O. ARM	72	28	137	54	1
I. BACK	138	54	114	45	1
O. BACK	61	24	76	30	1
BORDER	33	13	137	54	4

Cutting plan A: 7.5 m (25 ft)
Cutting plan B: 7.9 m (26 ft)

Before choosing a type of fabric, decide which way the fabric will go on the seat.
Cutting plan A requires it to have a join. With **cutting plan B** the fabric runs the
length of the seat. The pattern or pile of the fabric may determine the fabric's
placement. If it's going to be joined, then it may be possible to tuck the join down
between the back and seat.

Make sure that you have enough material. Take the widest points for any of the
components' measurements and add on an extra 3.8 cm (1.5 in) between each deep
button. Allow enough fabric for all the tuck-ins needed – for example, the length
will have to go through the gap between the seat and the back to the outside rail.

The fabric on the arm has a join which is best done through a button. Note that
the width from the corner near the back to the end of the arm can be deceptive.

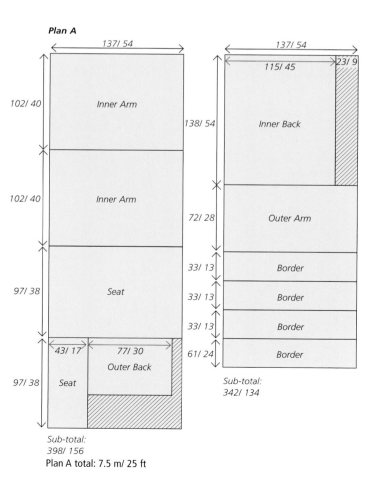

Plan A

137/ 54

102/ 40 — Inner Arm

102/ 40 — Inner Arm

97/ 38 — Seat

43/ 17 Seat | 77/ 30 Outer Back

97/ 38 — Seat

*Sub-total:
398/ 156*
Plan A total: 7.5 m/ 25 ft

137/ 54

115/ 45 | 23/ 9

138/ 54 — Inner Back

72/ 28 — Outer Arm

33/ 13 — Border
33/ 13 — Border
33/ 13 — Border
61/ 24 — Border

*Sub-total:
342/ 134*

Plan B

137/ 54

102/ 40 — Inner Arm

102/ 40 — Inner Arm

72/ 28 — Outer Arm

33/ 13 — Border
33/ 13 — Border
33/ 13 — Border
33/ 13 — Border

*Sub-total:
408/ 160*
Plan B total: 7.9 m/ 26 ft

137/ 54

97/ 38 — Seat

180/ 70

115/ 45

137/ 54 — Inner Back

77/ 30 Outer Back

61/ 24

*Sub-total:
379/ 148*

Index

Credits

Photographs on pages 12, 32, 116-117 courtesy of Jane Churchill Fabrics & Wallpapers (copyright: Jane Churchill Fabrics & Wallpapers).

Pages 7, 13, 31, 33 courtesy of Osborne and Little (stocklist number +44 (0)20 7352 1456).

Page 25, photolibrary.com

Other photographs and illustrations are the copyright of Quarto Publishing plc. While every effort has been made to credit contributors, Quarto would like to apologize should there have been any omissions or errors – and would be pleased to make the appropriate correction for future editions of the book.

Quarto would also like to thank the following companies for supplying sample fabrics and tools:
Osborne and Little (www.osborneandlittle.com)
Nina Campbell (www.ninacampbell.com)
Laura Ashley (www.lauraashley.com)
Glover Bros., Taunton

US consultant
Patricia Gilkey, Second Chance Upholstery, a San Francisco Bay Area upholsterer for 20 years, vetted member and five-year Director of the Association of Master Upholsterers and Soft Furnishers, widely acknowledged as the trade association of the professionals.